厦门大学哲学社会科学
繁荣计划资助项目

Storytelling in NatuRally Occurring Conversation

自然交谈中故事叙述的会话分析

·彭　欣　著

厦门大学出版社
XIAMEN UNIVERSITY PRESS
国家一级出版社
全国百佳图书出版单位

图书在版编目(CIP)数据

自然交谈中故事叙述的会话分析:英文/彭欣著.—厦门:厦门大学出版社，2019.6
ISBN 978-7-5615-7449-2

Ⅰ.①自…　Ⅱ.①彭…　Ⅲ.①会话—叙述学—研究—英文　Ⅳ.①H09

中国版本图书馆 CIP 数据核字(2019)第 102380 号

出 版 人　郑文礼
责任编辑　王扬帆

出版发行　厦门大学出版社
社　　址　厦门市软件园二期望海路 39 号
邮政编码　361008
总 编 办　0592-2182177　0592-2181406(传真)
营销中心　0592-2184458　0592-2181365
网　　址　http://www.xmupress.com
邮　　箱　xmup@xmupress.com
印　　刷　厦门集大印刷厂

开本　720 mm×1 000 mm　1/16
印张　11.25
插页　2
字数　260 千字
版次　2019 年 6 月第 1 版
印次　2019 年 6 月第 1 次印刷
定价　50.00 元

本书如有印装质量问题请直接寄承印厂调换

厦门大学出版社
微信二维码

厦门大学出版社
微博二维码

Preface

This book studies the organization of storytelling in Chinese conversation, with a focus on co-participants' practices in 'suspending' and 'returning' to storytelling sequences. The two aims of the study are: (1) to examine non-minimal responses from an unknowing story recipient during storytelling, which may 'sidetrack' the course of current telling; (2) to examine the storyteller's practices in getting back to the halted story and the interactional functions of managing a returning to the halted story.

The current study follows the analytical framework of conversation analysis. The analysis is based on 17 conversations between Mandarin Chinese speakers totaling about 450 minutes. Over 140 storytelling sequences are identified among which about 100 cases involve brief or longer side sequences after which the telling is resumed.

The findings reveal that a number of responsive actions from the story recipient may sidetrack an ongoing story with at least a two- or three-turn side sequence. Such recipient actions may briefly halt the progression of the telling, e.g. a question requires the teller to attend to the issue being pursued by the recipient in the next turn; a collaborative completion or predicting what might happen next in the story often makes the teller's confirmation/rejection relevant in the next turn; a display of stance or understanding may either minimally lead to the teller's acknowledgement or an exchange of views. Moreover, the momentary diversion may become more elaborated if local contingencies arise during the side sequence or if the initial turn of the side sequence is itself designed as prelude to upcoming actions.

It is found that the recurrent strategies used for story return include repetition of some element of the story near the point of interruption or direct continuation tying back to where the storyline was interrupted. Repetition is a more explicit cohesive device to tie back to the interrupted story as it locates the point to which the resuming telling is returning. In the case of direct continuation, returning is often prefaced by *ranhou* 'and then' serving as a 'tying-back' device. In addition, returnings may also be proposed by the storyteller who, while still in the side sequence, uses *fanzheng* 'anyway'—prefaced utterances to manage closure of the side sequence. When the side sequence becomes lengthy and complex, returning to prior telling may require more explicit indicator such as resuming search. Sometimes the storyteller may have to compete for tellership to get back to the interrupted story.

Further analysis shows that the interactional import of returning to halted story goes beyond merely pursuing the completeness of the story. As storytelling often implements certain actions in interaction, its suspension also suspends the course of action designed to implement. So returning to halted storytelling is a means through which the storyteller carries on the course of action which was put on hold with the halted story.

By documenting the recipient response that affects the course of storytelling, the storyteller's practices in doing return and the possible interactional import that motivates the returning, this study fills the gap in our knowledge of how participants co-organize storytelling in Chinese conversation. The study also contributes to conversation-analytic studies with the use of Chinese conversation data and provides basis for comparative studies of storytelling across languages and cultures.

Contents

Chapter 1

Introduction

This book studies the organization of storytelling in Chinese conversation using the conversation analytic approach, with a focus on co-participants' practices in suspending and returning to storytelling sequences.

In everyday conversation, participants often share with each other their own past experiences, or knowledge of past events, e.g. stories they learned from reading books, listening to news, or watching television, etc.. Conversational participants may also tell each other stories about themselves or others on various occasions, such as at friends' parties, family reunion, and classmates' gatherings. Or even when people walk to school or have a break during work, they may exchange with each other about what happened to them on the day before. In addition to storytelling in daily conversation, people often tell their stories in various institutional settings, such as in hospital, in courtroom, in therapy, in business conference where they recount their own experiences or what they witnessed. As a pervasive phenomenon in human social interaction, telling stories has been a research object of scholars from various disciplines for decades, such as in anthropology (Ochs & Capps, 2001; M. Goodwin, 1997), communication studies (Mandelbaum, 1991, 1993, 2010), psychology (Bruner, 1986, 1990, 2002; Sarbin, 1986), and sociolinguistics (Labov, 1972; Labov & Waletzky, 1967; Polanyi, 1985; Norrick, 1997, 1998, 2000, 2004, 2013). As sociolinguists Thornborrow and Coats (2005) put it, there is not much need to prove the significance of studying storytelling (narrative) in social sciences in the sense that storytelling is "central to the fabric of social interaction" (p. 1).

Studies on stories or narratives attracted scholars' attention early in the 1960s when Labov and Waletzky investigated ordinary people's stories (1967). With the use of narratives solicited in sociolinguistic interviews, Labov's (1972) description of the internal structure of narratives has been influential in that stories in real talk began to draw researcher's attention. However, in their line of inquiry, the analytical focus is on the speaker's narration; the responses made by the recipient of narratives (e.g. interviewer/researcher) are not taken into consideration. In other words, the concern then was not on narratives or storytelling as an achievement in social interaction. As pointed out by Schegloff (1997), there is nothing interactional in this form of analysis of narratives.

Started from another perspective, conversation analysis (henceforth CA) not only examines a different type of data for research (stories in naturally occurring conversation in contrast to those elicited in interviews), but also treats conversational storytelling as possible means to accomplish actions in talk-in-interaction. In other words, studies in CA show that storytelling in conversation may implement various social actions. For instance, Sacks points out that to tell a story is not just simply recounting what happened before without any reason but can be used to do something as it often has an "enormous amount of power" (Sacks, 1995b, pp. 286 & 469). Schegloff (1997) explicitly states that speakers can use stories to do a range of things, such as complaining, boasting, informing, alerting, teasing, explaining, and justifying in talk-in-interaction. Instead of focusing on the internal structure of stories (or narratives) in conversation, research following the CA approach examines the organization of storytelling from an interactional perspective and has established that storytelling is an interactively and collaboratively achieved activity, and the story recipient's participation is consequential to the actual course of telling. For example, whether a potential story can be launched and how it will be told has much to do with how (potential) recipient(s) respond to the proposal of the telling and what epistemic status they have with regard to the story to be told; when the teller is taking an extended turn to tell the story, the recipient may either make continuers such as *mm hm* and *uh huh*, or requests for more details about the story told so far; and the recipient may display his/her understanding or stance towards the story upon the story completion.

Earlier studies in CA have examined story beginning and ending (C. Goodwin,

1984; Jefferson, 1978; Sacks, 1974, 1978, 1992), but the telling sequence itself is a relatively less researched area. However, the recipient response during the speaker's extended turn (including but not limited to storytelling) has been researched, e.g. recipients' continuers (C. Goodwin, 1986; Jefferson, 1981; Schegloff, 1982), questions (Koike, 2009; Mandelbaum, 1987, 1989; Monzoni & Drew, 2009; Ochs & Capps, 2001), byplay (M. Goodwin, 1997), second stories (Sacks, 1995; Siromaa, 2012), and body behaviours such as gaze (C. Goodwin, 1984) and nodding (Stivers, 2008). Among this range of the recipient response, some appear to be more passive, e.g. continuers which indicate the recipient's passing of the opportunity to take a full turn with topical talk. Some of them may shape the course of telling in relatively more substantial way, e.g. the story recipient's byplay may subject the on-going story to the risk of being aborted so that the teller would make an extra effort in avoiding byplay to become the focal activity (M. Goodwin, 1997). Another form that may also largely influence the telling sequence is the recipient's questioning turn. As examined by Jefferson (1972), these questioning turns (other-initiated repair, questioning repeats, etc.) may trigger side sequence when the main sequence is going on. The recipient-initiated side sequence within an ongoing telling may be a brief one or it may develop into a quite lengthy and complex one. This makes the study of the organization of conversational storytelling apart from its beginning and completion point a challenging task as how a story may develop once begun appears fluid, contingent and hard to capture.

As side sequence often occurs in the telling sequence, a return may also happen subsequently (Jefferson, 1972). A number of scholars have studied 'return to prior' (e.g. prior talk, prior activities) as a general phenomenon, and documented patterns and lexical devices used in getting back to prior talk or activities (Ottesjö, 2005; Koenig, 2005; Local, 2004; Mazeland & Huiskes, 2001; Rauniomaa, 2008; Sutinen, 2014). A return to the previously suspended telling is also examined in English and Japanese conversation (Sutinen, 2008; Yasui, 2011). They focus on devices that speakers use in tying back to suspended telling. Drawing on Chinese conversational data, this book investigates the 'return' after a suspension in telling. In addition to examing practices used in doing return or facilitating the realization of a return, the interactional import of doing story return is also explored.

As there is still a lack of systematic and focused study on conversational storytelling in Chinese (except Kuo, 2002; Zhao & Zhao, 2014), this study is an initial step towards this direction. The particular research questions addressed in this study, i.e. recipient-initiated side sequence and storyteller-initiated story return, are two related phenomena within the telling sequence. By examining them together, this study is an attempt to explore the organizational and interactional aspects of the telling sequence for understanding how the teller and the recipient co-organize storytelling in Chinese conversation. It is hoped that the findings of this study contribute to conversation-analytic studies in Chinese conversation and provide basis for comparative studies of storytelling across languages and cultures.

The arrangement of this book is as follows. In Chapter 2, previous studies are reviewed. First, the definition and characteristics of conversational storytelling is discussed. Second, studies of the story recipient's epistemic statuses and their responsive actions are reviewed. The third part is a review of studies relevant to the phenomenon of returning. In Chapter 3, the procedure of conducting this study is introduced. The procedures of data collection, transcription, and analysis followed in this book are also presented. Chapters 4 and 5 are two main chapters presenting the analysis and findings of the research. Chapter 4 examines recipient-initiated side sequence. It starts with a sketch of two formats of recipient-initiated minimal side sequences within the telling sequence. Then various recipient actions that occasion side sequences are analyzed and described. The third part of the chapter presents analysis of side sequences expanded from the minimal format as a result of sequence design or interactional contingencies arising from the course of side sequence. Chapter 5 examines the storyteller's practices in 'returning' to suspended story. Specifically, this chapter presents analysis and findings of the linguistic resources employed by the storyteller such as repetition and direct continuation in tying back to his/her story halted or sidetracked by the side sequence. Possible interactional motivation of returning is also discussed in this chapter. Chapter 6 summarizes the findings and contributions of the study and concludes the book.

Chapter 2

Literature review

2.1 Introduction

In this chapter, I review previous studies on conversational storytelling in CA, focusing on the characteristics of storytelling, story recipients' epistemic statuses and their responding actions, the occurrence of side sequences, and the organization of storytelling resumption that occurs during the course of storytelling.

In Section 2.2, I review certain characteristics of conversational storytelling. Previous studies have differentiated conversational storytelling from narrative, telling, and other types of big-package telling. In Section 2.2.1, I review how conversational storytelling is differentiated from other frequently used terms. Then, I review relevant studies that focus on the social actions implemented by storytelling (Section 2.2.2). Following this, I discuss the turn-taking organization of storytelling. That is, in Section 2.2.3, I look at how the turn-taking system in conversational storytelling is distinctive from the turn-taking organization in ordinary conversation. Subsequently, in Section 2.2.4, I introduce the consequential sequences of storytelling. The last aspect I review is the interactive nature of storytelling in conversation.

As previous studies have shown, conversational storytelling is not a single-handed activity accomplished solely by a storyteller, but it is interactive in nature and involves the story recipients' co-participation. In Section 2.3, I first review previous studies that investigate the epistemic status of story recipients (Section 2.3.1). Then, in Section 2.3.2, I review studies on the story recipients' responding actions. In addition to the story recipients in story preface/beginning and ending, I also focus on the story recipients' responding during the telling sequence.

Previous studies also have shown that story recipients' responding actions may possibly put the ongoing telling on-hold and thus lead to the occurrence of a side sequence (Jefferson, 1978). In Section 2.4, I first review studies which examine side sequences triggered by story recipients' responding actions (Section 2.4.1). As the story halted by side sequence may be resumed on certain occasions, in Section 2.4.2, I review studies relevant to the phenomenon of return in general and return in storytelling.

2.2 Characteristics of conversational storytelling

In this section, I introduce and differentiate the definition of conversational storytelling from similar terms such as narrative, conversational narrative, and telling. Then, I discuss key characteristics of storytelling, including the social actions implemented through storytelling activities, its particular turn-taking organization, its consequential sequences, and the interactive nature of storytelling.

2.2.1 Storytelling

Regarding the frequently employed terms, Mandelbaum (1987) states that "terminologically, 'narrative', 'narration', 'discourse', 'story', 'anecdote', and 'storytelling' are used interchangeably" (p. 35). However, the term narrative usually puts stronger emphasis on the teller's work, as narrative refers to "monologues, preconceived and produced by a teller alone" (p. 59). The classic studies of narratives, which have mainly focused on tellers' works are Labov and Waletzky (1967) and Labov (1972).

Labov (1972) defines narrative as "one method of recapitulating past experience by matching a verbal sequence of clauses to the sequence of events, which (it is inferred) actually occurred" (pp. 359-360). After examining a collection of narratives, Labov identifies the internal, overall structure of narratives, including abstract, orientation, complication action, evaluation, result/resolution, and coda (p. 363). Schegloff (1997) notes that Labov and Waletzky's (1967) study is important in the sense that it attracts attention to "the interest of ordinary persons' stories of personal experience" (p. 98).

The internal structure of narratives identified by Labov has been influential in the sociolinguistic study of narratives. Labov and Waletzky (1967) use sociolinguistic interviews, and a large amount of narratives occur in their interviews. In their study, the researcher asked participants to describe their experiences in particular, extreme situations they had experienced. For example, the researcher asked participants questions such as, "What was the most important fight that you remember?" (p. 358) and "Were you ever in a situation where you were in serious danger of being killed?" (p. 363). After the interviewer asked the questions, the participants began to tell their stories. As summarized by Ochs and Capps (2001), the characteristics of this form of narrative are more likely to have "one active teller, highly tellable account, relatively being detached from surrounding talk and activity" (p. 20). In other words, the storyteller is highly entitled to talk despite his or her surrounding environment and regardless of how the interviewer/researcher responds to their stories. From Schegloff's (1997) perspective, this form of narrative has "nothing interactional in the data" (p. 101). Specifically, Schegloff (1997) points out that Labov and Waletzky (1967) report nothing about the recipients in the course of the narratives nor upon the completion of the narratives, and they do not report the details of the production of narratives such as the silences in the course of the narrative and the narrator's hesitations or hitches.

Starting from another perspective, Ochs and Capps (2001) focus on narratives in ordinary conversation, namely conversational narratives. When they investigate narratives in ordinary social exchanges, they take the recipients' actions into consideration. They find that, compared with narratives, conversational narratives often have the following characteristics: the narrative may have more than one possible active teller, the teller may have a moderately tellable account, and the narrative would be situated in the current social interaction. Kuo (2002) also examines narratives in daily conversation, although her definition of narrative is rather broad, including any recounting of a past event (both personal narratives and narratives of vicarious experiences). Specifically, personal narrative refers to narratives in which "the narrator is the major or minor figure," and narratives of vicarious experiences involve the "recounting of movie plots or newspaper reports, and stories about someone the teller knows" (p. 134). Kuo's (2002) use of narrative is similar to what Ochs and Capps (2001) called conversational narrative.

To briefly summarize: earlier researchers, such as Labov and Waletzky (1967), use narratives when focusing on the teller's work. However, recently scholars such as Ochs and Capps (2001) and Kuo (2002) have investigated narratives in ordinary conversation, and they not only approach the investigation from the teller's perspective but also take the recipients' responding actions into account. In this sense, conversational narrative and conversational storytelling, which are usually used in CA are similar to each other.

Schegloff (2007) states that storytelling is one of the common modes of telling and telling is "a generic type of activity in talk-in-interaction" (p. 43). As a generic form of activity, telling can be trouble-telling, joke-telling, storytelling, announcements, noticings, etc.. With regard to its organization, telling can either consist of a single utterance or of a long spate of talk that has many parts (Schegloff, 2007). Tellings are not just doing activities such as announcing, sharing noticings, and recounting experiences, per se. Rather, they can be vehicles for accomplishing other social actions. Schegloff (2007) gives two examples to illustrate this point. For instance, when someone says, "You're standing on my foot," the speaker is not just doing a telling, but also making a complaint. Schegloff (2007) says that through this telling, the speaker expects "more response than the news value and a sympathetic receipt or a remedy" (pp. 74-75).

Storytelling, as one form of a general telling activity, also takes many of its properties. For instance, a speaker can tell a story of his or her past experience in a single utterance. Or, his or her experience can also be elaborately recounted across a rather extended turn (or several turns) that consists of many more utterances. In storytelling, the speaker may also attempt to implement certain social actions, such as complaining, justifying, and substantiating, which we discuss in detail in the next section.

What follows is a comparison of storytelling and another form of large-packaged telling, i.e. trouble-telling. As one form of big-package activities, trouble-telling refers to people's talking about their troubles. Studies on trouble-telling have been conducted mostly by Jefferson (1980, 1988) and by Jefferson in collaboration with Lee (1981). Although Jefferson (1988) identifies the sequential order of trouble-telling's components, she also notes that trouble talk and other big-packaged tellings do not have "step by step explicit and overt training" as in other interactional practices, such as in greetings, question-and-answer sequences, telephone openings and closings (p. 439). The fact that there is no fixed way to tell stories is also true to the organization of storytelling activity in the sense that its realization also depends on its interactional contingency (Jefferson, 1978).

Compared with storytelling, trouble-telling is more specific as it refers to people's talk about trouble. While, for storytelling, the topic goes beyond 'trouble' and has a broader scope. Although trouble-telling and storytelling are different in certain aspects, both of their actual trajectories are contingent to their interactional context and both of them are situated in ongoing conversations.

As observed by Sacks (1978), stories are carefully placed in conversation, and their occurrence usually fits into the conversation. Jefferson (1978) also explains that a story can be "triggered in the course of turn-by-turn talk" (p. 220).

I have shown how the term storytelling is different from other terms, such as narrative, conversational narrative, telling, and trouble-telling. It is hoped that better understanding of the term storytelling in conversation can be reached through reviewing relevant studies. It is shown that most characteristically, storytelling is a big-package, socially ordered activity in which the teller usually recounts one's various sorts of experiences (or events), and its actual realization and sequential organization are highly contingent to the local interaction. More importantly, conversational storytelling involves both the storyteller's and the recipient's co-participation. When identifying and selecting storytelling sequences in recorded conversation, I use the above notion as a working definition.

2.2.2 Social actions implemented through storytelling

As noted earlier, Schegloff (2007) points out that a telling activity can be the vehicle for other social actions. This is also true for storytelling. Sacks (1995b) states that storytelling involves an "enormous amount of power" (p. 286). As to what stories can do, he points out:

> [t]hey're not, then, doing simply telling of a story for no good reason, or telling of something that happened once, or telling of something that happened once to somebody else, or that happens to people, but they're offering something that does something now, i.e. describes, explains, accounts for, our current circumstances—mine, or yours, or mine and yours (Sacks, 1995b, p. 469).

Sacks' study is perhaps the first to examine the telling of past event/experience in relation to what it can do for the participants in the current ongoing conversation where the telling takes place. In line with Sacks, Schegloff (1997) explicitly states that people can use stories to do a range of things, such as complaining, boasting, informing, alerting, teasing, explaining, and justifying.

In addition to these concrete social actions that can be implemented through storytelling, storytelling can also become an "interactional environment" in which the above social actions can be implemented (Schegloff, 1997, p. 97). For example, Sacks (1995b) shows that by using a story to share one's opinions, a person can thereby avoid a recipient's immediate fierce disagreement (pp. 285-286). Within the argumentative sequences in mundane conversation among children, as M. Goodwin's (1993) study shows, storytelling can provide boys and girls with "participation frameworks" so that they can construct and reconstruct their social organizations (p. 110). Specifically, the boys in M. Goodwin's study used stories to continue working on an argument while the girls used stories to restructure alignments of participants, both in the current interaction and in reference to a future time.

In the following, I use the story told in M. Goodwin's (1993) boys' group to illustrate how the interactional environment is provided through storytelling. Prior to the extract below, there is a counter sequence between the two boys, Tony and Chopper. From lines 19 to 25, Chopper is telling a story about Tony to the other participants present in the conversation.

(2-01) Extract from Example 5 in M. Goodwin (1993, p. 114)

12 Tony: I'm a dingy your head:d.=How would you
13 like that.
14 (0.4)
15 Chopper: No you won't you little-*h Guess what.
[Recognizable Counter to Prior] ↑ Self Interrupt [Story Preface]
Recognizable Counter to Prior *Self Interrupt* *Story Preface*
18 (0.4)
19 Chopper: Lemme~tell~ya.=Guess what. (0.8) We
20 was coming home from practice, (0.4)
21 and, three boys came up there (.) and
22 asked~us~for~money~and~Tony~did~like~
23 this. (0.6)

24 *hh ((raising hands up))
25 "I AIN'T GOT n(h)(hh) [o(m(h)oney)."
26 Pete: [Ah~hih~ha,

Here, as analyzed by M. Goodwin (1993), Chopper's story first ended the counter sequence (see line 15 where Chopper self-interrupts). Then it creates another participation framework, which was different from the one provided by the previously ongoing counter sequence. In telling the story, Chopper characterizes Tony as a coward who raised his hands (line 24) and said "I AIN'T GOT n(h)(hh) o(m(h)oney)" (line 25). M. Goodwin (1993) comments that in switching from the counter sequence to a story about Tony, the storyteller Chopper provides a participation framework where other co-participants could participate through, e.g. evaluating the reported event. In other words, the telling of the story provides an occasion where the other co-participants are also able to take sides in the dispute between Chopper and Tony, instead of being outsiders to their counter sequence.

To briefly summarize, telling a story is not just reporting a past experience/event. Storytelling can serve as a vehicle for carrying various social actions, and can provide appropriate interactional environment for such social actions.

2.2.3 Turn-taking in storytelling

The "bland fact" of storytelling uncovered by Sacks (1995b) is that "stories routinely take more than one utterance to do" (p. 222). That is, usually one or more parties attempt to tell the story for an extended series of utterances. And the story recipients, most of the time, do not talk in a substantial way.

With regard to the turn-taking of storytelling, Jefferson (1978) writes, "stories emerge from turn-by-turn talk, and upon their completion participants re-engage in the turn-by-turn talk" (p. 220). In other words, during storytelling, the turn-taking arrangement of ordinary conversation as identified by Sacks, Schegloff, and Jefferson (1974) (henceforth SSJ) is temporarily suspended.

Before going to the details of the turn-taking system in storytelling activity, I first review the classic study of the turn-taking system in ordinary conversation.

SSJ (1974) propose a model of turn-taking organization in daily conversation and characterize this model as "locally managed, party-administered, interactionally controlled, and sensitive to recipient design" (p. 696). According to Clayman's (2013) summary in an introductory chapter about turn-construction units and the transition-relevance place, SSJ's (1974) insight about turn-taking system in ordinary conversation is that "a speaker, upon launching a turn, has primary rights to the floor and the transfer of speakership becomes a salient possibility only at certain specifiable junctures" (p. 151). As each turn-constructional unit (TCU) is "recognizable in context as 'possibly complete,'" upon the completion of each TCU a transition-relevance place (TRP) is established (Clayman, 2013, p. 151). In each TRP, the change of speakership becomes relevant. The following sketch from Clayman (2013, p. 151) highlights the association between TCU completion and transition relevance, and also the contingent nature of turn transfer:

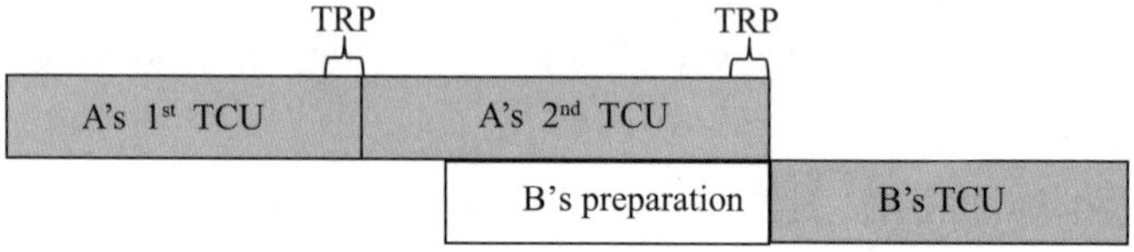

As shown in the above sketch, when A's first TCU reaches the first completion point, the first TRP is opened up and thus a turn transition becomes relevant. But as A continues to speak with the second TCU, a turn transition does not occur. When A's second TCU comes to its completion, a second TRP is opened up. In the meanwhile, if B intends to take up speakership, he/she starts to prepare for it before A's TCU reaches its completion so that he/she can start talking as soon as the second TRP is opened up. In other words, the turn-taking system in ordinary conversation only assigns one TCU to the current speaker once, and the turn transition becomes relevant when this TCU reaches its completion and a TRP is opened up.

Whereas, for the turn-taking in storytelling, Jefferson in her earlier study (1978) has indicated the insight that stories are occasioned in the turn-by-turn talk and then participants re-engage in this turn-by-turn talk upon the completion of the story. In addressing the question, "what makes a story recognizable as a story to recipients and to analysts?" Mandelbaum (2013) points out that when the teller begins to take an extended turn and the recipient passes the opportunity to take a turn, a storytelling can be recognized. In addition, she also states that "a suspension of the ordinary turn-taking arrangement of conversation" (p. 493) can be another important characterization.

Here, I use an example from C. Goodwin's (1984) to briefly show the turn-taking organization of storytelling.

(2-02) Extract from C. Goodwin (1984, pp. 225-226)
1 (4.0)
2 Ann: Well- ((throat clear)) (0.4) We coulda used a
3 liddle, marijuana, tih get through the weekend.
4 Beth: What h[appened.
5 Ann: [Karen has this new hou:se. en it's got
6 all this like- (0.2) ssilvery: g-gold
7 wwa:llpaper, hh (h)en D(h)o(h)n sa(h)ys,
8 y'know this's th'firs'time we've seen this
9 house.=Fifty five thousn dollars in Cherry
10 Hill.=Right?
((Lines 11-24 in the original extract are not included.))

According to C. Goodwin's (1984) analysis, Ann's utterance in lines 2 and 3 is a typical story preface, offering a story to tell. In line 4, the co-participant Beth makes a request to hear Ann's story, giving the go-ahead signal for Ann's potential storytelling. After getting the go-ahead signal, Ann begins to tell the story (line 5). She continues to tell the story about Karen's new house through line 10. Here, we can see that Ann's story takes more than one single utterance. That is, after Ann is granted the floor, she is entitled to take an extended multi-unit turn.

2.2.4 Sequential components of storytelling

As storytelling in conversation is usually a big-package activity, it can consist of certain components (Sacks, 1978). Stories are considered to be a designed organization, and they do not occur by accident (Sacks, 1986).

Regarding the beginning of storytelling, Jefferson (1978) not only points out that stories are locally occasioned from the ongoing conversation, but also explores how talk preceding storytelling is related to it. She finds that the potential storyteller uses varied devices, such as a "disjunct marker," an "embedded repetition," or their combinations (p. 221). In addition, storytellers also use a format typified by the expression "speaking of x" as a device in initiating or introducing a storytelling (p. 244).

Another explicit way the storyteller uses in introducing a story is story preface (Sacks, 1978). The purpose of the story preface is to "announce that there is a story coming" (Sacks, 1995b, p. 18). For instance, the expressions "Say did you see anything in the paper last night" and "I heard something wonderful today" are typical preface tokens in English conversation (Sacks, 1995b, p. 18). Sacks mainly concerns with the techniques of doing story preface, e.g. what goes into the preface that projects an upcoming telling, and how it solicits co-participant(s)' collaboration in granting the telling. In line with Sacks, C. Goodwin (1984) also gives his analysis on story preface. Instead of using the term story preface, he employs preface/request sequence which includes "a preface" indicating the attempt to tell a story and "a request" by the co-participants displaying interest to hear the story (p. 226).

In addition to story beginning and story preface, both Sacks (1974b) and Jefferson (1978) closely examine the ending part of storytelling. For instance, Sacks (1978) points out that upon the completion point of storytellers' telling the story recipient may display their understanding or make affiliative uptakes. One more story-ending device is an assessment or an evaluation of the story (Jefferson, 1978). For the conjunction between the story ending and its subsequent talk, Jefferson (1978) writes that, the ending of a story has the potential to trigger particular talk or actions or activities following it and this potential is the story's nature of sequential implicativeness.

For the overall organization of storytelling, Sacks (1974a) uncovers three "serially ordered and adjacently placed types of sequences" (p. 337), including the preface, the telling, and the response sequence①. However, Sacks does not mean that each instance of storytelling does necessarily contain all three sequences as he states that it is "incorrect to propose that given the initiation of some particular preface, a telling and a response sequence are sure to occur, or to occur without other materials intervening" (p. 337). Nevertheless, Sacks' insight provides a profound foundation for exploring the organizational structure of storytelling, i.e. how storyteller as well as recipient(s) organize storytelling for themselves in the interaction they are engaged. For example, C. Goodwin (1984) goes into a more detailed characterization of story components in the telling sequence as he states that background, climax, and parenthesis constitute the

① The response sequence here refers to the story recipient's response upon the story completion.

body of a story.

The study on 'telling sequence' is still a less researched area perhaps exactly because how the telling would progress is complex and relatively less constrained as its beginning and ending. In the present study, I particularly investigate the story recipients' non-minimal response which may occasion a halt of the ongoing telling and how the halted telling may be resumed.

2.2.5 The interactive nature of storytelling

In this section, I review studies about the interactive nature of storytelling. In general, stories are told to story recipients. What is characteristic of conversational storytelling is that it is often locally occasioned, contingent on the ongoing interaction and requires collaboration from co-participants who agree to position themselves as recipients for the duration of the telling. In other words, storytelling is a joint achievement of both the teller and the recipient. The teller and the recipient work together in the launch, progression and completion of the telling. In this section, I specifically review its interactive nature from two aspects. First, the emergence of storytelling is relevant to the local interaction of the ongoing conversation. Secondly, storytelling is not a single-handed activity of the storyteller alone. Instead, the story recipients also participate in the whole process of storytelling, once they recognize it as a story.

According to Jefferson (1978), stories emerge from and are occasioned by the turn-by-turn talk. Similar to Sacks' notice on the emergence of a certain utterance, according to Jefferson (1978), "the occurrence of an utterance at a given moment is accountable" with reference to its prior utterance (p. 220). A storytelling occurrence is also accountable as stories are interactionally relevant to the ongoing conversation.

Jefferson (1978) documents two aspects of the local occasioning of stories. First, she notes that "a story is 'triggered' in the course of turn-by-turn talk" (p. 220). The mention of something in a given conversation by one participant might remind another participant of a particular story that "may or may not be topically coherent" with the ongoing conversation (Jefferson, 1978, p. 220). Second, Jefferson (1978) also shows that stories are "methodically introduced" (p. 220) when specific techniques such as a disjunctive marker "Oh" and an "embedded repetition" are used, and when they display the relationship between the story and its prior talk (p. 221). In addition, these techniques employed in introducing stories also account for and propose the appropriateness of the storytelling.

In addition to the aspect that stories are occasioned by the ongoing turn-by-turn talk, the interactive nature of storytelling is also exhibited in the storyteller's and the recipients' participation in the whole storytelling process. In addition to Mandelbaum's (1987) and C. Goodwin's (1984, 2013) explicit proposal that storytelling is an interactive activity between the storyteller and the recipient, many studies have shown that story recipients' responsive actions are of great significance in the sense that recipients' participation influences the progression of storytelling.

As I mentioned in Section 2.2.4, Sacks (1974) identifies three serially ordered sequences in storytelling, namely, the preface, the telling, and the response sequences. Although Jefferson (1978), Schegloff (2007), and Sacks (1995a, 1995b) all point out that not all stories necessarily begin with story prefaces, Sacks' (1974b) three identified storytelling sequences provide a sequential order so that we can follow how a storyteller and the recipients interactively construct the storytelling.

The story preface, which is a pre-sequence to the telling of a story, usually carries a range of functions. One of the issues a story preface deals with is the potential storyteller's need to check whether the upcoming story is known to the potential story recipient (Schegloff, 2007). Furthermore, a story preface can be designed to give a characterization of the upcoming story, enabling the potential story recipients to know what the upcoming story will be and what kind of response they could make upon the story's completion. Responding to a story preface, the story recipient may produce a 'go-ahead' or a 'block' signal, allowing or not allowing the launching of the story. After getting the go-ahead from the potential story recipients, the storyteller can begin the story. However, if the potential teller gets a 'block' from the potential recipients, the storyteller might choose to abort the upcoming story, or he or she might adjust the potential story to get a 'go ahead.'

The following is an example of how a potential recipient responds to the story preface, illustrating how the realization of a story is achieved interactively. Here, I use C. Goodwin's (1984) example again (labelled as 2-03 below) to show the occurrence of a story preface and the potential story recipient's response to it.

(2-03) Extract from C. Goodwin (1984, pp. 225-226)

(4.0)
Ann: Well- ((throat clear)) (0.4) We coulda used a
liddle, marijuana, tih get through the weekend.
Beth: What h[appened.
Ann: [Karen has this new hou:se. en it's got
all this like- (0.2) ssilvery: g-gold
wwa:llpaper, hh (h)en D(h)o(h)n sa(h)ys,
y'know this's th'firs'time we've seen this
house.=Fifty five thousn dollars in Cherry
Hill.=Right?
((Lines 11-24 in the original extract not included here.))

In this extract, Ann produces a typical story preface, offering to tell a story (lines 2-3). This is responded to by Beth with the question "What happened" (line 4) which gives Ann a go-ahead signal. By giving the go-ahead, Beth displays (1) her understanding that Ann is proposing a storytelling, and (2) her alignment to the proposed telling by giving the turn back to Ann thus positioning herself as the recipient of the upcoming story. The above example shows how the potential storyteller and recipient negotiate with each other before the teller can get an extended turn.

As the recipients recognize the potential story, and if they endorse it, typically, they relinquish the right to possible speakership upon completion of each TCU for the duration of the telling sequence, thus endorsing the teller extended turn space with multiple TCUs. That is, during the telling sequence, the storyteller is entitled to construct his/her talk with more than one TCU for a period of time. However, this does not mean that story recipients do not produce any talk. In fact, they do produce talk, understood as responses to the story being told, in the telling sequence. They place various forms of responses to the telling, such as continuers (e.g. "mm hm" and "uh huh"), comments, queries, and sarcastic remarks (Sacks, 1995a, pp. 684 & 766). Sacks explains that recipients are not barred from talking during the telling sequence. Their display of attention, understanding, and stance, etc. or bid for solving hearing or understanding problems actually enjoy the "intended lawfulness" of the "interruptive status" (Sacks, 1974b, p. 345). In other words, recipients' talk can be seen as built in the organization of storytelling which keeps confirming recipiency for the benefit of the storyteller. Sacks' insightful observation on the status of recipients' talk in the telling sequence brings out the interactive nature of storytelling. Studies focusing on recipients' talk will be reviewed in Section 2.3 below.

As storytelling will have to come to its completion, story recipients are expected to produce appropriate responses to show their recognition of story completion and their understanding of what the story is about. Sacks (1995b) finds that one business of a story recipient is to produce appreciation of the story upon recognizing its completion. The appreciation tokens such as the expressions "[h]ow nice" and "[o]h that's too bad" constitute an understanding of the point of the story (p. 766). Or recipients may produce summary-like utterances to show what their understanding of the story is, as illustrated in Sacks' extract presented below.

(2-04) Extract from Sacks (1995b, p. 422)
Roger: She's doing that 'cause all'er friends're (doin' it).
(//) over th'Beadles.
Louise: Mm they need some kinda idol y'know, something to / / look
up to,

In a sense, story recipients are accountable to recognizing story completion and displaying such recognition at the 'right' place, i.e. the place they produce understanding of the point of story is the place where the teller has indeed finished telling. Failure to do so may be noticeable as illustrated in Jefferson's extract presented below.

(2-05) Extract from Jefferson (1978, p. 233)
01 HARMON: I said "And-and-and" "What ih-" "Is her boyfriend a nice
02 ma: n Joey?" He sz "Oh he's very nice, he's a colored man."
03 hhh*hhhh* [*H A H* hah!
04 LIL: →a Oh no::: the poor kid yer [kidding.
05 HARMON: [I said-
06 HARMON: →b No waita second I said "Joseph, that's, not your mother's
07 boyfriend. That colored man is the man ( ) she -
08 eh he takes her tuh work every day.
09 LIL: Uh huh.
10 HARMON: This colored man. [( )-
11 LIL: [Sure- What difference does it make, sure

As can be seen, at Arrow a, the story recipient Lil obviously treats what have been told so far by Harmon as the completion of the story when she responds with "Oh no::: the poor kid yer kidding" (line 4). However, Harmon explicitly rejects it as premature by saying "No waita second" (Arrow b) followed by further telling. It is at line 11 when more is heard that Lil shows her understanding of a now possible complete story by producing an adjusted response based on what has been told up to that point.

To briefly summarize, storytelling in conversation is interactive and collaborative in nature. Story recipients play an important role in each phase of the storytelling sequence. What they respond to the proposal and progression of the telling is consequential to whether and how the story would be told, and whether they appropriately recognize story endings is also accountable. In the next section, I review relevant studies on story recipients.

2.3 Story recipient

As I reviewed previously, story recipients work together with tellers in shaping storytelling in conversation. That is, recipients' responses to story prefaces are consequential to whether a proposed story would be told or how it would be told; recipient's minimal responses during storytelling, such as continuers at the possible completion of turn-constructional units, are good evidence that they recognize and endorse the teller's need of extended multi-unit turn for their stories (C. Goodwin, 1986; Schegloff, 1982); and the story recipients participate in negotiating what a story amounts to. Storytelling in conversation has been recognized as an interactively organized activity that is jointly achieved by both the storyteller and the recipient (C. Goodwin, 1984; Mandelbaum, 1987, 2013).

As story recipients are also different from each other in their epistemic statuses, they may make different responses. In this section, I first review studies relevant to the story recipients' cpistemic statuses and then the specific responding actions made by the story recipients.

2.3.1 Epistemic status

Story recipients vary according to their epistemic statuses with regard to the story being told. Story recipients who know about the event (C. Goodwin, 1979) or who have also experienced the same event (Sacks, 1995b) are characterized as "knowing recipients." Recipients who are aligned as or "not expected to know about an event being reported" are referred to as "unknowing recipients" (C. Goodwin, 1979, p. 100).

First, the recipient's epistemic status is consequential to whether a story would be launched, and how it would be told if launched. For instance, story preface (pre-announcement) can be designed to avoid reporting events already known to a knowing recipient (Schegloff, 2007; Terasaki, 2004). Tellers may also construct their utterance to accommodate both the unknowing and the knowing recipients (C. Goodwin, 1979).

The following is a classical example from C. Goodwin which shows how a speaker refines his utterance to accommodate recipients who have different epistemic statuses.

(2-06) Extract from Goodwin (1979, p. 98; lines re-arranged)

01	John:	I gave, I gave up smoking cigarettes::. = ((gazing at Don))
02	Don:	= Yea:h,
03		(0.4)
04	John:	I- uh: one-one week ago t'da:y, acshilly, ((gazing at his wife Beth))

The extract is taken from a conversation among two couples: John and Beth, and Don and Ann. In line 1, John tells Don that he has given up smoking cigarettes. When producing this utterance, John directs his gaze at Don, who, as a guest visiting John and Beth, apparently has no knowledge of the change in John's status as a smoker. Then, in line 4, John continues his previous utterance from line 1 and adds a time adverbial—"one week ago today." When John produces this utterance, he directs his gaze towards his wife, Beth, who obviously knows the event being reported. C. Goodwin (1979) argues that John's initial utterance (line 1) is designed for an unknowing recipient, Don, the visitor, but not Beth, his wife, since there is no point reporting an event that his wife has already known. However, when John adds the phrase "one week ago today" (line 4), the event that John has given up smoking is re-cast as a different event: it is not simply a good news worth reporting but worth celebrating now that the day of the conversation is a kind of anniversary (i.e. a 7-day anniversary of giving up smoking). The re-cast of the event makes the reporting appropriate to the knowing recipient, Beth. This example well explicates how a speaker can refine his or her utterances to accommodate both unknowing and knowing recipients.

Second, previous studies have also found that story recipients with different epistemic statuses shape the ongoing story in different ways. For instance, knowing recipients often monitor the telling of the story (Sacks, 1995a), and may become co-tellers themselves (called "story consociate" by Lerner 1992). They may initiate repair if they spot trouble in the telling, or they may provide another version of the story, join in the telling (recipient-turned storyteller), and proffer an invited collaboration, etc. (Beach, 2000; C. Goodwin, 1986; Lerner, 1992; Mandelbaum, 1987). Lerner (1992) identifies and describes a set of entry devices for story consociates to assist storytelling. He finds that story consociates may be asked to join in the telling when the current teller experiences some problem in moving the telling forward. Or, entry into the current telling may be initiated by the story consociates themselves when they see troubles in the telling regarding, e.g. event sequencing of the story, delivery and elaboration of the story, or facts in the story. The following is an example that shows how the story consociate enters the story through repairing a trouble in event sequencing.

(2-07) Extract from Lerner (1992, pp. 261-262)

01	Tim:	so I said (I said y'know) an' whadda you think I aughta do?
02	Melenie: →	well FIRST he didn['t say anything for a long time
03	J:	[(boy ya better send that o(h)ne)
04		(.)
05	Melenie:	you kinda foldit up we threw the rest a the mail away you just
06		kinna fo:l didit up an carried it up stairs

According to Lerner's (1992) analysis, here, Melenie's "well FIRST," in line 2, locates what Tim says in line 1 as an "out of sequence" (p. 262) component in the story. As a knowing recipient, Melenie not only repairs the trouble but also takes this opportunity to assume tellership as can be seen in her further talk in lines 5-6.

Besides, unknowing recipients also monitor the telling, but in ways different from the knowing recipients and thus shape the progression of the story in different ways. A typical contribution from the unknowing recipients is perhaps their questions (this is not to say knowing recipients do not ask questions). Questions from unknowing recipients have been examined in conversations in Japanese (Koike, 2009, to be reviewed below in Section 2.3.2) and Italian (Monzoni and Drew, 2009). The following example from Monzoni and Drew's (2009) study shows one unknowing story recipient's questioning turn in storytelling. As their data is in Italian, I use the English translation.

(2-08) Extract from Monzoni and Drew (2009, pp. 201-202)
01 CI: when we married, Lucio (1.0) bought =
02 CI: = the mirror of the bathroom with the two sconces.
03 (1.4)
04 RE: → aren't you divorced yet Cinzia?
05 (1.8) ((Ci. is eating and towards the end of the gap she nods her head))
06 CI: I forgot to! =
07 RE: =[that's it exactly- =
08 FE: =[yes be careful! = [because in this home
09 CI: = [HAHH. HAHH. HAHH.
10 FE: [(?one) the wives.=
11 RE: [because- because I-
12 RE: =because I and she were married in the same month.
13 RE: and we divorced uh:::m the same month.

Monzoni and Drew (2009) point out that RE's question (line 4) comes at the moment when CI is apparently unable to forward the telling (as evidenced by the long pause at line 3). It shows how an unknowing recipient, who doesn't know what the storyteller will tell, can intervene in the ongoing story in particular sequential and interactional context, and does so in a humorous way. In this excerpt, although RE's question in line 4 appears to be a request for clarification, actually RE knows that CI is not divorced; thus RE's question is seen as a 'wise-crack,' designed to distort CI's reference to her marriage.

In this section, I have reviewed previous studies relevant to the story recipients' epistemic statuses. As there are relatively fewer studies examining unknowing recipients' responding actions in the literature, the present study aims to fill the gap by focusing on unknowing recipients' responsive actions, particularly when such actions halt the ongoing telling sequences.

2.3.2 Recipients' responding actions

Previous studies have shown that the story recipient produces a range of responses, such as continuers, assessments (C. Goodwin, 1986), questions (Koike, 2009; Mandelbaum, 1987, 1989; Ochs & Capps, 2001), byplay (M. Goodwin, 1997), second stories (Sacks, 1995a, 1995b; Siromaa, 2012), and body behaviours such as gaze (C. Goodwin, 1984) and nodding (Stivers, 2008). Some of the responses, such as continuers, assessments, and questions, are seen as being on a continuum from passive to active, depending on the extent to which they shape the course of the telling sequence (Mandelbaum, 2013).

For instance, C. Goodwin (1986) explicates the difference between a continuer and an assessment. Continuer (e.g. mm and uh huh) displays "recipient's understanding that an extended turn at talk is in progress but not yet complete and also recipient's collaborating in the achievement of that multi-unit utterance by passing the opportunity to either (a) produce a more extended turn of their own or (b) initiate repair on the talk just heard" (p. 207). The recipient's doing of an assessment, however, is not "simply acknowledging receipt of the talk just heard" but "assesses what was said by treating it as something remarkable" (C. Goodwin, 1986, p. 207). The following example illustrates the story recipient's producing of a continuer and an assessment during the telling sequence.

(2-09) Extract from C. Goodwin (1986, p. 206)

01	Hyla:	One time I member, .hh 's girl wrote
02		end her, .hh she wz like (.) fifteen er
03		six[teen end] her mother doesn let'er wear
04	Nancy:→	[Uh hu:h,]
05	Hyla:	.hh nail polish er sh(h)ort ski:::rts
06		'er:[:: .hhhhhh]
07	Nancy:→	[Oh: wo:w] =
08	Hyla:	= Oo::h no I remember what yesterday was

Here, the storyteller Hyla takes an extended turn to tell the story (lines 1-3). Nancy's utterances of "Uh hu:h" (line 4) and "Oh: wo:w" (line 7) are a continuer and an assessment, respectively. According to C. Goodwin's (1986) analysis, although they share certain characteristics, such as they occur in a similar environment (during the telling sequence), continuers and brief assessments are different in certain respects.

For example, assessments usually have lexical content while continuers often do not. Continuers such as "Uh huh" are more likely to be restricted in certain places. That is, they are more likely to occur "in the midst of extended talk by another" (C. Goodwin, 1986, p. 214), while assessments can occur both in the midst of another's extended talk and upon the possible completion of a story. Specifically, when a story recipient treats a certain place as story completion, she or he will not produce a continuer. Regarding the continuer produced by story recipients, Stivers (2008) explicates that story recipients' vocal continuers show their alignment to the storytelling's structural organization.

In addition to continuers and assessments, story recipients' questions have also been researched. For instance, Mandelbaum (1987, 1989) shows how a story recipient plays an active role in eliciting and directing a storytelling through questioning turns. The example below shows the story recipient actively participates in the storytelling activity and moves the storytelling forward in a turn-by-turn fashion.

```
(2-10) Extract from Mandelbaum (1987, p. 15)
47   A:      I'm so ti:yid. I j's played ba:ske'ball
48           t'day since the firs' time since I wz a
48a          freshm'n in hi:ghsch[ool.]
49   B: 1→                       [Ba::]sk(h)et=
50           =b(h)a(h)ll? (h) [(Whe(h)re.)
                    [(Nnhnh hnh)
51   A:             [Yeah fuh like an hour
51a          enna ha:[lf. ]
52   B:               [.hh]
53   B: 2→   Where didju play ba:sk[etbaw.   ]
54   A:                             [(The) gy]:m.
55   B: 3→   In the gy:m? [(hh)
56   A:                   [Yea:h. Like group therapy.
57           Yuh know [half the grou]p thet we had=
58   B:               [Oh:::.        ].hh
59   A:      =la:s' term wz there en we [jus' playing
59a          arou:nd.
```

Here, the recipient elicits the story, and thus the story proceeds in a turn-by-turn fashion triggered by the series of questioning turns as indicated by the three arrows

(Mandelbaum, 1987). A's utterance from lines 47 to 48a projects a telling about A's tiredness after playing basketball. However, B does not align with the theme of "tiredness" proposed by A. Instead, B insists on focusing on the basketball theme as indicated by Arrows 1 and 2. After B's third question at Arrow 3, the storyteller, A, produces a more extended turn about the story of playing basketball. Here, A's story is carried on in a turn-by-turn format in which B is largely responsible for the direction the story progresses.

Using Japanese conversation data, Koike (2009) also investigates story recipients' questions. By examining recipient's questions asked in various phases of storytelling sequence, e.g. in the pre-telling, the story preface, the telling, and the post-telling sequences, Koike shows how story recipients' questions function in their eliciting, repairing, forwarding, expanding, extending, or digressing a storytelling. In addition, Koike also explores story recipients' questions in joint storytelling where a story is collaboratively told. He shows that the story recipient keeps monitoring the teller (co-teller), and the participation framework changes when a story recipient initiates questions.

Another recipient response, byplay, is examined by M. Goodwin (1997). It includes "teasing, heckling, or playful dealing with a description of the story" (p. 78). She finds that through producing byplay, participants may open up a floor that occurs simultaneously to the main floor but is subordinate to it. The storyteller and the principally addressed recipient need to handle and treat the byplay. M. Goodwin (1997) points out the worth of studying the story recipient's possible forms of responses as they not only "promote the teller's rendering," such as by including side comments or heckling. These aspects also draw Sacks' (1974a) attention as these different forms of responses display the recipients' different alignments in the telling sequence.

Recipient's non-verbal responses such as gaze and nodding have also been researched. For example, C. Goodwin (1984) examines the gaze organization of storyteller and recipient with regard to various story sequential positions. Stivers (2008) explicates that story recipient's vocal continuers "simply align with the activity in progress and nods claim access to the teller's stance toward the events" (p. 31).

Producing a second story is another kind of recipient response which is more substantive in the sense that it requires more turn space as a telling in itself. Sacks (1995a) notes that hearing other people's tellings about something might remind someone of his or her own experience. They may produce a second story which "very nicely picks up the point of the first" (p. 767). This entails that the teller of the second story, who was the recipient of the first, has analysed what the teller of the first was saying in that story. A recent investigation by Siromaa (2012) shows that a first-story recipient may produce a second in ways that resonate with the first in structure, lexical-syntactic choice and prosody. Siromaa argues that such resonance is both a method to anchor the second story in relation to the first and a resource to display stance. A resonating second story manifests an interpretation of the first story and also proffers a new perspective on the first story, from which the first story's import may be refined, redefined, or rejected. In the meanwhile, in producing the second story, the former story recipient becomes the current storyteller. Transforming from recipient to teller also shows that participants' role in storytelling is not fixed but fluid.

Through different ways of responding, story recipients can either deal with the business of "displaying understanding" and "affiliative takes" (Sacks, 1978, p. 261) or they might show their alignment and affiliation to the storytelling in progress (Stivers, 2008). However, some responsive actions from recipient may be potentially interruptive in the sense that they may halt or derail a current telling, either very briefly or in more substantial ways. For example, when a recipient asks a question about one detail of the story and the teller turns to produce an answer the progression of the telling would in effect be suspended. On certain occasions, the suspended telling may be resumed. Studies on this phenomenon is reviewed in the next section.

2.4 Side sequence and the phenomenon of returning

Jefferson (1972, p. 294) is perhaps the first to notice "side sequence within an ongoing sequence" when she examines the sequential organization of a break in an ongoing activity. Following her pioneering work, other scholars (including Svennevig, 1999; Koenig, 2005) have also conducted studies on side sequence. In 2.4.1 below, I review studies on side sequence.

When Jefferson (1972) analyses side sequence within an ongoing sequence, she also notes and documents the phenomenon of returning, i.e. how speakers go back to the sequence which has been suspended by the side sequence. Recently, this phenomenon has attracted increasing attention. Many scholars have studied returning as a general phenomenon, and documented patterns and lexical devices used in returning to prior talk or activities (see Ottesjö, 2005; Koenig, 2005; Local, 2004; Mazeland and Huiskes, 2001; Rauniomaa, 2008; Sutinen, 2014). Other scholars have studied returning specifically in conversational storytelling and identified devices that speakers use to get back to suspended storytelling (Sutinen, 2008; Yasui, 2011).

In Section 2.4.2, I review the previous studies of "returning," in both general environments and in conversational storytelling.

2.4.1 Side sequence

Jefferson (1972) is the first to use the term "side sequence" and she characterizes it in the following way:

> In the course of some on-going activity (for example, a game, a discussion), there are occurrences one might feel are not "part" of that activity but which appear to be in some sense relevant. Such an occurrence constitutes a break in the activity - specifically, a "break" in contrast to a "termination"; that is, the on-going activity will resume. This could be described as a "side sequence within an on-going sequence (p. 294).

Jefferson documents various forms that participants repeat and interrogatives that might trigger the occurrence of a side sequence. She notices that various forms of repeats from the recipient of an ongoing sequence (such as questioning repeats, laugh-token repeats, and affirmative repeats) and their questions (such as "Who?" and "What?") that target certain objects in the telling may trigger a side sequence and thus temporarily stop the ongoing sequence.

Svennevig (1999) furthers study on side sequence in his investigation of conversations among people on their first encounter. He documents side sequences which are initiated by either a recipient or the speaker him/herself. Four central characteristics of side sequence are identified by him (Svennevig, 1999, p. 259):

1. A side sequence constitutes a suspension of the on-going joint project.

2. The task carried out in the side sequence is not part of the main project, but is relevant to (parts of) it. The relation may be either one of sequential implicativeness or merely a parenthetical relation. It may be either anaphoric or cataphoric.
3. The main project resumes once side sequence is complete.
4. The side sequence consists minimally of one interactional contribution (presentation and acceptance), but may include a series or sequence of turns.

In Svennevig's terms, Jefferson's "on-going activity" (p. 294) is called "the original joint project" (p. 259). The "original joint project" can also be referred to as a "main project" or a "main sequence" (p. 259) which is clearly distinguished from a side sequence. He also specifies "break" in Jefferson's terms (p. 294) as "a suspension of the main sequence," caused by "a rupture in the coherence or the projected action sequence" (p. 259).

Furthermore, he has also investigated certain communicative functions of side sequences such as repair sequences, monitor sequences, digressions, misplaced sequences, and resource scanners. For instance, a repair sequence locally deals with "projections of the local sequence" (p. 305), while monitor sequences serve to establish solidarity, such as to mitigate face threats. Digressions and resource scanners are more likely to pursue purposes such as adding or soliciting relevant personal or biographical information relevant to the current topic, establishing community affiliation, etc..

Examining a similar phenomenon, Koenig (2005) investigates question-initiated oblique sequences. Oblique sequences are characterized as a sequence within the main (ongoing) sequence and are initiated by the recipient of the ongoing talk. An oblique sequence can be relevant to the main sequence but not necessarily "in furtherance of" it (p. 2). Koenig (2005) not only schematizes the sequential organization of oblique sequences, but also documents the interactional functions that oblique sequences implement, such as to show surprise, to ask for additional information, and to challenge.

2.4.2 The phenomenon of returning

As Jefferson (1972) schematizes in her study, the sequential organization of the side sequence within on-going sequence is: (O)-(S)-(R), representing on-going sequence, side sequence, and returning to ongoing sequence, respectively. She also differentiates two ways of doing returning, namely "resumption" and "continuation" (p. 318). These two means of returning have their own distinctive components and techniques. For resumption, the speaker makes an extra effort, such as by using attention getters (for example, "Listen" or "Hey, you know"), which explicitly signal an upcoming returning. Jefferson also remarks that "resumption marks that there is a problem in accomplishing a return" (p. 319). However, for continuation, the speaker does not need to do additional work in getting back to the previous on-going sequence; rather, the speaker proposes that "there is no trouble" so that he or she can carry on the previous on-going sequence as if it had not been suspended (p. 320). Jefferson also finds that connectives such as "and" and "so" can be initial components in continuation. As Local (2004) comments, although there is no extensive technical specification of continuation and resumption in Jefferson's study, her pioneering work is influential on later studies of this phenomenon.

Following Jefferson's line of study, Mazeland and Huiskes (2001) investigate resumption in two environments, after repair-sequence expansions and after competing lines of topic development. Their study shows that the Dutch word *maar* ("but") can be used as a resumption marker. The use of *maar* in the turn initial position can first tie the current talk back to the earlier talk and thus establish a relationship with the prior context. In addition, resumption initiated with this lexical item precedes another TCU where the resumed talk is continued. Mazeland and Huiskes (2001) identify two construction formats, [*maar* + recycling abandoned telling] and [*maar* + return to the start of the topic], as patterns of practice that speakers use in returning to suspended prior talk. However, this does not mean that Mazeland and Huiskes treat *maar* as a specific lexical item in doing resumption. Instead, they argue that the fact that the *maar* utterance which precedes the recycling of an earlier utterance or returning to the previous topic determines *maar*'s resuming property.

Local (2004) also notices a similar phenomenon that certain utterances do not link to immediately preceding utterances, but tie back to earlier utterances produced by themselves. Local finds that the utterance and-uh(m) can be used as a back-connecting device to get back to prior talk, and it has distinctive characteristics regarding its sequential position, strategic deployment, and phonetic features. Particularly, Local shows that this turn-beginning and-uh(m) has a cluster of stable phonetic properties, such as its characteristically quieter volume than surrounding talk, and its relatively level pitch, etc.. He further points out that the utterance and-uh(m) implements an interactional work to propose continuing the prior action.

When examining the organization of oblique sequences, Koenig (2005) explicates the devices employed by speakers in implementing a return to what occurred before the oblique sequence. He points out that in addition to the return itself, there is an optional component, namely the "pre-return" (e.g. "well anyway"), which can set aside the oblique sequence and signal an imminent return (p. 20). Regarding the specific techniques in doing the return, Koenig also differentiates between resumption and continuation. He specifies resumption as speakers' repeating or rephrasing some elements in the TCU before the oblique sequence, and continuation as their directly producing a TCU as a next in relation to the utterance before the oblique sequence.

Using Swedish conversational data, Ottesjö (2005) also examines linguistic resources used in continuing and resuming communicative projects, such as a report of the preparations of a trip or a Christmas list. Focusing on various coherence-creating practices, Ottesjö finds that the utterance *iallafall* ("in any case," or "anyway") is a resumption marker and that *så* ("so" or "then") can signal a continuation of the prior project (e.g. narrative). As Ottesjö's research (2005) is written in Swedish, the brief mentioning of her work here is based on the accompanying summary in English provided in her thesis.

Using both Finnish and English data, Rauniomaa (2008) also examines how repetition is used by the speaker to accomplish a return to prior talk. Sutinen (2014), on the other hand, examines the "resuming" of suspended activities such as games, using Finnish data. Her focus is on the negotiation that happens when doing resuming.

As a brief summary of what I have reviewed to this point: most of the scholars have focused on the lexical items that introduce a return (e.g. Mazeland and Huiskes, 2001; Local, 2004; Koenig, 2005; Ottesjö, 2005) as they examine returns at various levels, such as to prior talk, to prior communicative projects, etc.. In the following I review two studies which focus on returning in storytelling: Sutinen (2008) and Yasui (2011).

In Sutinen's (2008) master's thesis, she investigates the resumption strategies employed in storytelling and other extended turns, such as descriptions and explications. She examines resumptions subsequent to both self-initiated and other-initiated digression and finds that together with repeating or recycling elements from a previously on-going story, the discourse markers but and anyway serve as resumption markers.

Specifically, she demonstrates the ways in which but and anyway serve as resumption resources in various contexts, such as after digressions triggered by self-initiated repairs and during joking sequences and other initiated information requests, comments, repairs, joking sequences, and challenges.

Starting from a cross-linguistic perspective, Yasui (2011) focuses on projection in storytelling in her doctoral research. She finds that speakers employ certain vocal resources in projecting a return to an abandoned story, both in American English data and in Japanese data. In her study, she also makes a distinction between two forms of returning: continuation and resumption. Continuation in her study is characterized as "unproblematic return to an ongoing story; whatever suspended a telling is treated as a subsidiary part of a story"; and resumption as "problematic return to an ongoing story; whatever suspended a telling is treated as a digression" (p. 121). Her study shows that speakers use conjunctions such as "and" and "but" in American English and *de* ('and') and *dakedo* ('but') in Japanese as devices to project a continuation, while English *but* and Japanese *demo* ('but') can serve as "attention getters" (Jefferson, 1972, p. 319), and that they function as resumption markers here. Yasui (2011) provides a study of this phenomenon with more insights into how speakers resume an abandoned story.

2.5 Interim summary

As scholars interchangeably use terms such as narrative, conversational narrative, narrative, and telling, this chapter starts by reviewing previous studies on the definition of storytelling. Then I discussed certain crucial aspects of storytelling, such as its interactional functions, its turn-taking organization, its sequential organization, and its interactive nature.

As shown in Section 2.2, storytelling is not a single-handed activity by the storyteller alone. Rather, both the storyteller and the recipient work together to make storytelling happen as an organized activity. Thus, in Section 2.3, I mainly focused on previous studies that focus on story recipients, including their epistemic statuses and their responsive actions in the telling sequence.

Story recipients' responsive actions shape the telling of stories in different ways, and an on-going telling may be suspended by certain recipient's action and returned to later. In Section 2.4, I reviewed previous studies on the phenomena of side sequence and returning.

Storytelling as a big-package activity in conversation presents certain challenge in the study of its organizational structure and interactional functions. This may partially explain the relatively fewer studies of it within the field of CA where much advances have been made in other relatively smaller or more local sequences. To the best of my knowledge, systematic conversation-analytical study of storytelling in Chinese conversation is yet to be made. As an initial step to fill in the gap, the present study chooses to focus on side sequence and returning in Chinese conversation.

Chapter 3

Methodology and data

3.1 Introduction

This chapter introduces the methodology and data employed in the present study. Section 3.2 introduces the sort of data, transcription system, and analytic method used by conversation analysts; Section 3.3 introduces the data collected for the current study and describes my analytic process. Specifically, Section 3.3.1 presents a detailed explanation of the source population my data is drawn from, the data collection process, and basic information about each conversation. Section 3.3.2 introduces the case identification process and describes how each storytelling sequence was selected and analyzed. In Section 3.3.3, I give an overview of how the selected cases are used and presented in the subsequent analysis chapters.

3.2 Methodological issues in conversation analysis

As a research field with its root in sociology, CA was first developed by Harvey Sacks, Emanuel Schegloff, and Gail Jefferson in the 1960s at the University of California. The basic theoretical assumption of CA is that social interactions among human beings and social actions implemented in social interaction are organized in an orderly fashion. In this section, I will first introduce CA's data-based nature and its data transcription system. Then, I will describe how data is analyzed in this system.

3.2.1 Data and transcription

CA is a typical data-based methodology. Instead of using manufactured examples, conversation analysts base their theorizing of interactional phenomenon on collected data from naturally occurring human social interaction. The data is audio- or video-recorded so that analysts can repeatedly assess it. In the early days of CA, speech was the primary focus of study. Later, particular bodily behaviors such as nodding and eye gaze drew growing attention, especially in the work of C. Goodwin (1984). Nowadays, it becomes more common to apply multi-modal analysis to video-recorded data so that not only the verbal but also the non-verbal aspects of the interaction can be examined in much more detail.

Although CA is inductive in nature and has certain characteristics of the qualitative method, a large amount of cases or instances are required for analysis and generalization. As pointed out by Clayman and Heritage (2002), the simple characterization of CA as a qualitative method is "somewhat misleading" (p.19), since its practitioners consistently use large numbers of examples and examine these examples in a systematic way. However, CA is also different from quantitative studies in the sense that it still emphasizes the close analysis of individual cases (Clayman & Heritage, 2002). For instance, in Schegloff's (1968) early study on telephone openings, over 500 telephone conversations were studied in a case-by-case fashion before an analysis of the observed interactional phenomenon was offered.

In CA, conversation analysts use a transcription system developed by Gail Jefferson (Heritage & Atkinson, 1984). There are two main concerns in conversation transcriptions. First is the question of how to capture the turn-by-turn unfolding of talk-in-interaction in the transcripts. Overlaps and gaps among speakers, as well as pauses, latchings, etc. all serve certain communicative purposes and have consequential meanings embodied. To solve this problem, in the transcription system, all the conversation devices related to turn-taking are assigned specific symbols. A second concern has to do with speech delivery. Although Kelly and Local (1989) point out that CA has no set of systematic regulations for the transcription of phonetic properties (e.g. the accurate measure of lengthening, loudness, etc.), the main characteristics of speech delivery, such as stress, intonation, pitch, lengthening, etc. are transcribed in detail. In addition, details like laughter, in-breath, out-breath, etc. are also documented, as these characteristics have also been proven to have interactional significance.

This set of transcription conventions not only provides conversation analysts with a channel to transfer verbal utterances into written form, but it also ensures that details significant for the participants themselves in their sense-making of each other's talk such as pauses, lengthening, breathing, etc. are preserved. This detailed transcription system has been designed to support the theoretical assumptions and goals of CA by imposing a meaningful order throughout all aspects of the recorded conversation.

However, although the transcription system is crucial to analysis, conversation analysts do not base their analysis on written transcripts only. Rather, the transcripts are examined together with the recordings in their raw audio and video forms, since these recordings best document the naturally occurring social interaction among interactants.

3.2.2 Analytic methods

When analyzing the collected data, conversation analysts use a controlled method to work on the data episodes. Although analysts may have a hunch about an interactional phenomenon when they begin their research, the analysis itself is not based on intuition. Rather, it is the co-participants' orientation and interpretation that constitute the analysis that is the backbone of CA. As incisively pointed out by Schegloff (2007), if the analysis does not capture the co-participants' understanding displayed in subsequent turns, it is not a CA analysis. That is, the target and resource of CA analysis is co-participants' understanding, orientation and interpretation of what they have said to each other.

One typical analytic method used in CA is next-turn proof procedure. This analytic tool is also relevant to the methodological aspects of sequential organization.

In each pair of prior and subsequent turns, the latter turn (known as the "next" turn) shows how its speaker interprets the prior turn. Any prior turn may embody different possible actions that are largely determined by its composition (i.e. turn design) and position of that turn in the overall organization of a given sequence, and sets up certain expected reactions for the next turn. The next turn is then where its speaker displays his/her understanding of the prior and would be inspected as such by the speaker of the prior. Whether the interpretation displayed in the next turn is judged as a match or mismatch to what the prior turn's speaker intended to convey will then be displayed in the following turn by the prior turn's speaker.

The following example serves to illustrate how the participants follow the next-turn proof procedure in their interpretation of each other's talk.

(3-01) Extract from Hutchby and Wooffitt (2008, p. 14)

1	Mother:	Do you know who's going to that meeting?
2	Russ:	Who?
3	Mother:	I don't know!
4	Russ:	Ouh::prob'ly:Mr Murphy an' Dad said prob'ly
5		Mrs Timpte en some a' the teachers.

The mother's question in line 1 may lead to alternative interpretations, e.g. a request for particular information about the meeting or a pre-announcement of her own delivery of that information. In responding to the mother's question, Russ may either provide the requested information apparently asked for by the question or treat the mother's question as a pre-announcement by letting mother have the next turn for the projected announcement. In line 2, Russ produces another question, 'Who?' indicating that Russ is not treating his mother's question as a simple request for information but as a pre-announcement. By asking 'Who?', Russ is giving a go-ahead for his mother to have the next turn. However, mother's response 'I don't know' in the next turn (line 3) reveals that Russ' interpretation about his mother's question does not match his mother's intended action. By saying 'I don't know', mother provides a "proof" that she was not projecting an upcoming announcement but was making a request for information at line 1. What Russ says next in lines 4-5 also provides a "proof" of his adjusted understanding of mother's question at line 1 as he now provides the information he actually has about the meeting.

Next-turn proof procedure explicates an interpretive mechanism underlying participants' interpretation of each other's talk. It works between a prior turn and its next in a chaining fashion: as the interaction among participants unfolds on a turn-by-turn basis where each next turn becomes a prior when a new next turn is produced, next-turn proof procedure keeps working between each pair of prior and next. With this interpretive mechanism, participants constantly orient to, respond to, and analyze each other's talk. More importantly, the sequential positions of the produced turns are crucial for the speaker's co-participants to analyze and interpret. As pointed out by Heritage and

Atkinson (1984), when viewing sequential organization at the methodological level, the participant's understanding of each utterance is by reference to "its turn-within-sequence character" (p. 7), a resource that enables both the co-participants and conversation analysts to make sense of what has happened.

3.3 Data and analytic procedures

This section introduces the data used in the current study and the procedures for the analytical process. First, I will describe how the data was collected and provide basic information for each conversation. Then, I will introduce the case identification process and illustrate how the data is presented in the analysis chapters.

3.3.1 Data in the current study

The data for the present study comprises two sets of conversations between native speakers of Mandarin Chinese. The first set of data (the ES series) was obtained from a previous research project[②]. This set of data was collected in 2005 and consists of 11 two-party conversations with a total length of 3.5 hours. All the conversations were audio- and video-recorded in a sound-proof room for the sake of sound quality, and the participants talked with each other casually with no limitation on topics of the chat.

The second set of data (the SR series) was collected for another research project[③] for which I served as a transcriber. The recordings were made during April 2011 and Septemmber 2012, in three cities: Hong Kong, Shenzhen and Jishou[④]. This dataset consists of 19 face-to-face conversations running approximately 14 hours in total. All participants gave their consent[⑤] to be audio- and video-recorded. The conversations were recorded during participants' gatherings in dorms, common rooms, library discussion rooms, cafés, at home, etc.. Participants in both data sets were not aware of

---

② My gratitude to Prof. K.K. Luke and Dr. Zhang Wei.

③ General Research Fund awarded by Research Grants Council of Hong Kong [CityU 154311] to Dr Zhang Wei.

④ Hong Kong is the Special Administration Region of China after its handover in 1997. Shenzhen is a city in Guangdong Province which borders Hong Kong. Jishou is a city in Hunan Province to the north of Guangdong Province.

⑤ The consent form is in Appendix.

the current research question.

The present study is based on 17 conversations (from the above two datasets) running a total length of 7 hours and 32 minutes. The following is a summary of the data used in the current study.

Table 1 Summary of the first dataset

Data	Duration	Participants	Topics
ES-M01	21min25sec	FF	family members, research, sports
ES-M02	24min35sec	FF	visit home, dating, marriage, movie
ES-M03	21min17sec	MM	news, tragedy in university dormitory, tax, social problems
ES-M04	22min57sec	FF	a famous professor's class, Yuanren Chao, sociolinguistic class
ES-M05	19min50sec	FF	reunion among friends, book, movie
ES-M06	21min18sec	FM	majors, transportation in holiday, research
ES-M07	21min38sec	FF	experiment, holiday plan, travel
ES-M08	10min54sec	FM	sports, travel
ES-M09	17min47sec	FF	study tour plan, previous trip, air fares
ES-M10	27min54sec	FM	study, hometown, sports, work
ES-M11	21min31sec	FF	traveling experience

Table 2 Summary of the second dataset

Data	Duration	Participants	Topics
SR-M01	64min15sec (20min08sec)⑥	FF	traveling experience, graduation trip, intern
SR-M09	100min54 (33min03sec)⑦	FFF	traveling experience, accent, TV programs, jokes, celebrities
SR-M15	41min44sec	FF	romantic relationship, dating, personality
SR-M17	41min16sec	FF	sportsmen, TV show, TV series
SR-M18	40min15sec	FF	university life, study tour
SR-M19	43min49sec	FF	business, university life, TV show, intern experience, future career plan

⑥ In SR-M01, the data is transcribed till 20min08sec in the recording time.
⑦ In SR-M09, the data is transcribed till 33min03sec in the recording time.

3.3.2 Case identification and analysis

As the present study focuses on storytelling in conversation, the first step was to build a collection of storytelling sequences. Following the definition of storytelling given in Chapter 2, the 17 conversations were watched and listened to repeatedly and 147 cases of storytelling sequences were identified. The length of these sequences varies, from a rather short story that takes two TCUs, to stories that last more than ten minutes.

In analyzing this collection of cases, I strive to sketch a description of the particular phenomenon in question. The goal of this kind of description is to produce a generalized account for the whole set of instances.

Based on the collection of storytelling sequences, a case-by-case analysis was first conducted. During this phase, I examined each storytelling sequence for its turn and sequential organization. I first examined each case to identify ways in which stories emerge in the ongoing conversation. I then focused on the story recipient's response during the telling sequence, and examined how story recipients' actions shaped the progression of the storytelling. In particular, I examined those responses from recipients that led to a halting of a telling. In addition, I examined how storytellers return to a suspended story. That is, I investigated the overall sequential organization of each storytelling sequence and analyzed its unfolding moment-by-moment development.

3.3.3 Data presentation

I followed the transcription conventions developed by Jefferson (Atkinson and Heritage, 1984) in presenting the data. As the data is in Mandarin Chinese, utterances produced by participants were transcribed into Chinese characters. Repeated examination of the audio and video recordings was required in order to transcribe each conversation and refine the transcripts from time to time.

As is customary now, the presentation of the Chinese data in an English text is often made in a four-line fashion. The first line is the transcript of the recorded utterances in Chinese characters. The second line contains corresponding pinyin, a Chinese Romanization system, which gives a rough phonetic shape of the words in line 1 for non-Chinese readers. The third line provides a word-for-word gloss in English and the fourth line provides free English translation. Although the first line of Chinese characters does not seem necessary in an English text, it is included in this study for the benefit of bilingual readers whose native language is Chinese. The following is an illustration of data presentation in later chapters.

苏:	然后	我	就-	.h	我	就	管他的	我	>就<	说 =
Su:	ranhou	wo	jiu-	.h	wo	jiu	guantade	wo	>jiu<	shuo=
	then	I	just		I	just	whatever	I	just	say
	'and then I just- whatever I just said='									

3.4 Interim summary

In this chapter, the methodological framework of the present study was introduced. First, I introduced the kinds of data employed in CA studies, transcription system, and the analytic procedure used in CA. Then, I documented the data used in the current study. In addition, the case identification, analysis processes and the method of data presentation were described in detail.

Chapter 4

Recipient-initiated side sequence

4.1 Introduction

This chapter focuses on responses from story recipients in the course of storytelling that lead to the emergence of side sequences in storytelling.

As conversational storytelling is a joint activity, the actual progression of telling would be shaped and influenced by a range of story recipient's response. For instance, the recipient's response to the story preface is consequential to whether a proposed story will get told, and how it will be told; at the story's completion, the story recipient may make an evaluation; and while the story is ongoing, the recipient's minimal responses in the telling sequence, such as continuers, are produced to indicate to the teller that they recognize and endorse the teller's need for an extended, multi-unit turn for the story (C. Goodwin, 1986; Schegloff, 1982). Particularly, different types of recipient response produced within the telling sequence, such as continuers and questions, shape the ongoing telling in different ways. Continuers, such as *mm hm* and *uh huh*, display a relatively passive recipiency (Mandelbaum, 1987, 1993) as they mainly indicate a pass on "the opportunity to do a full turn at talk" (Jefferson, 1993; Schegloff, 1982, p. 91). The following example demonstrates the story recipient's production of continuers during the telling sequence. Prior to this extract, the storyteller Su has been describing how she decided to join her mother's tour group earlier.

(4-01) SR_M01_1318_Meet my mother [storyteller = Su; recipient = Yi]

01 苏： 我 想 早 一点 见 我 妈 嘛，=
Su: wo xiang zao yidian jian wo ma ma,=
I want early a.bit see my mother PRT

02 [然后 我 就 - .h 我 就 管他的 我 >就<说 =
[ranhou wo jiu - .h wo jiu guantade wo >jiu< shuo=
then I just I just whatever I just say
'I wanted to see my mother as soon as possible, = and then I just- whatever I just said='

03 易： → [mm
Yi: *[mm*

04 苏： = 好 谢谢 那 我 去 圣淘沙 找 你们，= 然后
Su: =hao xiexie na wo qu shengtaosha zhao nimen,=ranhou
ok thank then I go Sentosa find you then

05 [后来 我 就 自己 去 那里 吃 了 个 饭，
[houlai wo jiu ziji qu nali chi le ge fan,
later I just self go there eat ASP CL rice
'=OK, thank you, then I go to Sentosa to find you, =and then I just went there by myself and had a meal,'

06 易： → [mm
Yi: *[mm*

07 ((Su continues the story.))

Here, Yi's 'mm' (lines 3 and 6) produced during Su's telling does not affect the trajectory of the telling as it is brief and is not responded to by Su who continues her story without any pause. In this case, Yi's 'mm' is produced as a continuer which indicates relatively passive recipiency and is understood as such by Su, the teller of an ongoing story.

In contrast to producing minimal responses such as continuers, recipient may also produce other non-minimal responsive actions which may have a more substantial influence on the course of telling, e.g. by asking questions, doing other-initiated repairs, engaging in collaborative completion, etc.. Such responses are more likely to be overtly acknowledged by the storyteller and thus put the telling on hold as the current focal business of the teller would change from 'telling' to 'dealing with' the story recipient's response. As this happens, a side sequence would emerge which sidetracks the ongoing telling.

This chapter will first outline the sequential organization of a minimal 'side sequence' occurrence, occasioned by story recipient's non-minimal response (Section 4.2). Then I will present findings on the kinds of social actions that are implemented through the various recipient responses that can potentially trigger a side sequence (Section 4.3). Specifically, my findings show that certain kinds of responses are very likely to result in treatment by the storyteller — for instance, the story recipient's requesting for more details, their facilitative responses such as collaborative completion and prediction of a next story element, their display of a stance and understanding, etc.. These forms of story recipient response will be analyzed respectively in Sections 4.3.1 – 4.3.4. Finally, Section 4.4 summarizes the findings presented in this chapter.

4.2 Sequential organization of side sequence in telling sequence

As early as in the 1970s, Jefferson (1972) first noticed the phenomenon of "side sequence within an on-going sequence" in conversation (p. 294). When this happens, the progression of the main sequence, and therefore the focal activity being carried through that sequence comes to a break, at least for a brief moment, during which the contingencies that have triggered the side sequence become the focal business for the participants in the side sequence. When the focal activity of an on-going conversation is storytelling, side sequences may also occur, e.g. resulting from story recipient's response towards the telling-so-far. Extract 4-02 below illustrates the occurrence of a side sequence occasioned by an instance of other-repair.

Lena, the story teller in the extract, has been recounting her family's tour to many places in Beijing. She has just finished telling about their visit to the Great Wall, and at the start of 4-02 she is telling about their visit to other tourist spots including the Thirteen Tombs of the Ming Dynasty on another day during their stay in Beijing.

(4-02) ES_M11_0513_Thirteen Tombs [storyteller = Lena; recipient = Tina]

```
01   LEN:   我们    当时          是   下午        四十    度      唉 :, (.)
            women dangshi       shi  xiawu       sishi   du      ai :, (.)
            we     at.that.time be   afternoon  forty   degree PRT
02          .h 我们    先    是   去   参观      那个  :: (0.8)  十三：   水 -
            .h women  xian  shi  qu   canguan  na-ge :: (0.8)  shisan:  shui-
               we     first be   go   visit    that-CL          thirteen water
```

'When we were there it was forty degrees in the afternoon, (.).h we first went to visit tha::t (0.8) Thirtee:n water-'

03 (.)

04 TIN: → 十三陵 .=
shisanling.=
Thirteen.Tombs
'Thirteen Tombs.='

05 LEN: =哎 -, 十三陵 .=
= ai-, shisanling.=
INTJ Thirteen.Tombs
=*'Yeah-, Thirteen Tombs.'*=

06 TIN: =噢 .
=ao.
INTJ
'=Ao.'

07 ((Lena returns to her story.))

Extract (4-02) begins with Lena's description of the high temperature of the day (line 1). When she goes on to name the spot they first visited in the afternoon of that day, Lena seems to encounter some trouble in naming the spot right away as indicated by sound stretches of the filler *nage::* 'that::' and the first word of the place *shisan:* 'thirteen:' and cut-off on the word *shui* 'water' (line 2). Then Tina immediately initiates an other-repair on *shisan shui* 'thirteen water' by providing the correct name *shisan ling* 'Thirteen Tombs' (line 4). This is then accepted by Lena who repeats the correct name (line 5) and followed by Tina's sequence-closing third[⑧] (Schegloff, 2007) *ao* 'yeah' (line 6). Lena then resumes to storytelling in line 7 (not shown in the extract). The sequential organization of 4-02 can be schematically represented in the following.

Table 3 Sequential organization of other-repair initiated side sequence

Storyteller:	Ongoing storytelling
Recipient:	Other-repair
Storyteller:	Acceptance of other-repair
Recipient:	Sequence closing third
Storyteller:	Returning to halted telling

⑧ Sequence-closing thirds are "designed to move for, to constitute a minimal expansion after the second pair part", and "to propose sequence closing" (Schegloff, 2007, p. 118).

As shown in the schema, the suspension of the ongoing telling is occasioned by the story recipient's other-repair which develops into a three-turn sequence of its own. The focal activity of the two participants during the repair sequence is switched to working on the correct name of the tourist spot visited by the storyteller. Although the name of the spot is relevant to the telling, no further recount of the visit is given in the repair sequence. In other words, the telling of what happened next in the story is put on hold until the close of the repair sequence[9].

Extract 4-03 illustrates a similar sequential organization. The two participants here are Qi and Yue. Qi has been telling Yue that her boyfriend was very touched by the present she gave him but he himself was not romantic at all in giving presents.

(4-03) SR_M15_2505_Boyfriend [storyteller = Qi, recipient = Yue]

01	琪： Qi	他 跟 我 送 什么，=一个 台灯，(.).h °我° 气 死 了. ta gen wo song shenme,= yige taideng, (.).h °wo° qi si le. he with me send what one-CL lamp I mad die ASP
02		((拍手)) (.)他 还 说 挺 浪漫 的，那天 ((paishou))(.) ta hai shuo ting langman de, natian clap he even say pretty romantic PRT that.day
03		>寄过来<(.)我 说 °嘶:° 你 给我 买 什么，=>他 说<,= >ji-guolai<(.) wo shuo °si:° ni gei wo mai shenme,=>ta shuo< mail-COMP I say SOUND you for me buy what he say *'What did he send to me, = a desk lamp, (.).h this drove me mad. ((Clap))(.)He even said it's pretty romantic, he mailed it to me the other day (.) I said '°si:° what did you buy for me', =>he said<,='*
04	悦： Yue	=(哦-) =(o-) oh *'=(oh-)'*
05		(.)

⑨ Jefferson (1987) observed that other-repair can be initiated and carried out in an embedded manner in which the main activity continues without a side sequence. As the concern of this book is the effect of recipient-initiated side sequence on the course of storytelling, the embedded repair sequence is not considered. Other types of recipient response which does not lead to side sequence is also beyond the scope of this book.

06 琪: 因为- 我 告[诉 他:,
Qi yinwei- wo gao[su ta:,
because I tell him
'Because I told hi:m,'

07 悦: [mm
Yue *'[mm'*

08 悦: m[m
Yue *'m[m'*

09 琪: [我 虽然 这样 问 他，你 千万别 告诉 我，因为
Qi [wo suiran zheyang wen ta, ni qianwanbie gaosu wo, yinwei
I although this ask him you never tell me because

10 我 很 喜欢 追求 [惊喜.
wo hen xihuan zhuiqiu [jingxi.
I very like pursue surprise
'Although I asked him like this, you better never tell me, because I like the feeling of getting a surprise.'

11 悦: → [mm. 然后 他 告[诉 你 了.
Yue [mm. ranhou ta gao[su ni le.
then he tell you ASP
'mm. And then he told you.'

12 琪: [他 没 告诉 我.
Qi [ta mei gaosu wo.
he not tell me
'He didn't tell me.'

13 悦: 哦.
Yue o.
oh
'Oh.'

14 ((Qi returns to the previously halted telling.))

4-03 starts with Qi telling Yue that her boyfriend drove her mad when he sent her a desk lamp as present and said it was pretty romantic (lines 1 and 2). Qi then goes on to detail the conversation between her and her boyfriend on the day the desk lamp was sent to her. Qi told Yue that she asked her boyfriend what he had bought for her, but actually she would prefer him not to tell her because she would like to get a surprise (lines 2-3, 6, 9-10). Having heard earlier Qi's characterization of her boyfriend as an unromantic person (prior to the extract), and also Qi's stated preference for getting a surprise, Yue starts to predict the boyfriend's reply to Qi's question of what he had bought for her by saying 'then he told you' (line 11). Yue's prediction displays her expectation of what an unromantic boyfriend might do based on what she has heard so far. Predicting the next happening in the storyline can be supportive in nature as it can facilitate moving the telling forward. However, as the prediction comes from the recipient, it makes relevant the storyteller's confirmation or rejection as the next action. As it turns out, Yue's prediction is rejected by Qi who says 'he didn't tell me' (line 12) which is followed by Yue's acknowledgement (line 13). After this, Qi continues the story and told Yue what her boyfriend said about the present. In this case the side sequence is occasioned by the story recipient's predicting of the story line. It shows a similar sequential organization as 4-02, i.e. a recipient action leads to a three-turn side sequence which temporarily sidetracked from the main storyline. And this schema can be further generalized to include various recipient actions responsible for the start of the side sequence as shown in the following:

Table 4 A three-turn side sequence within telling sequence

Storyteller:		Ongoing storytelling
Recipient:	→	Side-sequence-initiating action
Storyteller:		Orienting to recipient's action
Recipient:		Sequence closing third (SCT)
Storyteller:		Returning to halted telling

As shown in the above two examples, a side sequence may have three turns during which a speaker's ongoing telling is put on hold. However, the storyteller may return to halted telling right after he/she has responded to the recipient action that occasioned the side sequence, i.e. upon completion of responding to the recipient's side-sequence-initiating action, the teller can return to the halted telling in the next TCU of his/her responding turn. This can be schematized as follows:

Table 5. Returning occurs immediately after storyteller's response

Storyteller:		Ongoing storytelling
Recipient:	→	Side-sequence-initiating action
Storyteller:		Responding to recipient action
		+ returning to halted telling

The following two examples follow the sequential arrangement schematized in table 5. Prior to extract (4-04), Li has been telling what her classmates learned in the course of 'History of Contemporary Literature' in a top university in China. Extract (4-04) begins with Rui's recounting of her own experience of encountering several people from department of Chinese on the internet.

(4-04) ES_M04_0148_Department of Chinese [storyteller = Rui; recipient = Li]

01 芮: e- 那 很 有意思 huh huh 昨天 我 还
Rui e- na hen youyisi huh huh zuotian wo hai
that very interesting yesterday I also

02 上网, 网 - 碰到 几个 中文系
shangwang wang- pengdao jige zhongwenxi
surf.the.net net meet several-CL department.of.Chinese

03 的 人, = 然后 在网上 发 帖子, =
de ren, = ranhou zaiwangshang fa tiezi,=
PRT person then on.the.Internet send post

04 [然后 -
[ranhou-
then
'That's very interesting, huh huh Yesterday I also got on the Internet, and met several people from the department of Chinese, and then (they) posted on the Internet, and then-'.

05 李: → [哪个 :: 学校 的 中文系 .=
Li [nage:: xuexiao de zhongwenxi.=
which-CL university PRT department.of.Chinese
'The department of Chinese in which university.'

06 芮: = 应该 - (0.3) 不 知道 因为 网上 嘛,=
Rui =yinggai- (0.3) bu zhidao yinwei wangshang ma,=
should not know because on.the.Internet PRT

07 然后 他们 就 说 他们 [是 中文系, =
ranhou tamen jiu shuo tamen [shi zhongwenxi,=
then they just say they are department.of.Chinese
'Should-, I don't know as it's on the Internet, and they just said they were from the department of Chinese,'

08 李: [> 哦 哦 <
Li [> o o <
oh oh
'oh oh'

09 芮 : =因为 他们 当年 学 了 什么，=
Rui =yinwei tamen dangnian xue le shenme,=
because they in.those.years learn ASP sth.like

10 中国 当代 文学 史 什么的，
zhongguo dangdai wenxue shi shenmede,
Chinese contemporary literature history and.the.like
'As they learned something like History of Chinese Contemporary Literature,'

11 ((Rui returns to the previously halted story.))

Rui tells Li that she met through the internet some students from a Chinese department who post messages on a website (lines 1-3). Just as Rui is continuing with the next bit in the telling (*ranhou* 'then' in line 4) Li simultaneously starts to ask *nage xuexiao de zhongwenxi* 'The Chinese department of which university' (line 5). This enquiry about the specifics of the Chinese department mentioned by Rui results in a side sequence where Rui turns to answer the question, and her own telling is thus halted for the side sequence.

Although Li produces a receipt token 'oh oh' (line 8), showing her accepting of Rui's explanation, Rui does not wait but continues to make use of the turn and adds more information about them and then continues to tell the story. That is, the story teller does not wait for the story recipient's proposal to close the side sequence. Rather, the story teller closes the side sequence by returning to the telling right after giving a response to the recipient action.

Extract (4-05) is a similar case. Prior to the start of the extract, Lena has been recounting her visit to many scenic spots when travelling in Beijing with her family.

(4-05) ES_M11_0553_Jing Shan Park [storyteller = Lena; recipient = Ruth]

01 Len: 故宫 我们 玩 了 三个 小时 大概 .
gugong women wan le sange xiaoshi dagai.
Forbidden.City we visit PRT three-CL hour about

02 [(0.6)[我们 是 从 后门 往 前门 走 的 .
[(0.6)[women shi cong houmen wang qianmen zou de.
we be from back.door toward front.door walk PRT
'We stayed in the Forbidden City for about three hours. (0.6) We walked from the back door to the front door.'

03 Rut: [.h [故 -
[.h [gu-
'.h Gu-'

04 (0.6)

05 Rut: 哦::[:,
O ::[:,

06 Len: [我们 先 去 的 那个 景山 嘛 .
[women xian qu de nage jingshan ma.
we first go PRT that-CL Jing.Shan PRT
'We first went to Jing Shan.'

07 Rut: .h 噢 对 .=
.h ao dui.=
INTJ right
'.h Ao right.='

08 Len: =.h 景山 然后 [翻过去 的 .
=.h jingshan ranhou [fanguoqu de.
Jing.Shan then climb.over PRT
'=.h Jing Shan and then we climbed over it.'

09 Rut: → [那个 -(.) 皇帝 的 后花 [园 .
[nage- (.) huangdi de houhua[yuan
that-CL emperor PRT private.garden
'That- emperor's private garden.'

10 Len: [对 对 对 .
[dui dui dui.
right right right
'Right right right.'

11 ((Lena returns to the halted telling.))

This extract starts with Lena's telling about their visit to the Forbidden City (lines 1 and 2). Lena continues to tell Ruth that they went to Jing Shan first (line 6) and then climbed over the hill (line 8). At this point Ruth comes in to proffer her knowledge of the history of the park, independent of Lena's telling, that it used to be the emperor's private garden. By doing so Ruth displays her recognition of the place (i.e. Jing Shan) that Lena is talking about, (line 9), and it also makes relevant Lena's confirmation or rejection. As it turns out, Lena ratifies with *dui dui dui* 'right right right' (line10) resulting in a two-turn sequence during which Ruth's recognition of the historical park becomes the focal activity. However, Lena quickly returns to her telling by immediately picking up from where it was halted right after ratifying Ruth's recognition display.

In this section, the basic sequential organizations of recipient-initiated side sequence in telling sequence is sketched. The two schemas given above show that a side sequence can be closed by the recipient whose SCT proposes no further topical talk thus providing for possible return to the halted telling. Or, the side sequence can be closed by the teller, who makes use of his/her own responsive turn in the side sequence to return to the halted telling after first giving a relevant response to the recipient's action that sidetracked the telling.

Although side sequences may develop into quite extended ones due to contingencies emerging during the side sequence or as a result of sequence design, these will be examined in Section 4.4.

In the following, the recipient actions that may sidetrack the main telling sequence will be examined in more detail.

4.3 Recipient actions that occasion side sequence

My data shows that when the story recipient orients to the story told so far and makes a response, he/she is implementing one of a number of forms of social action — requesting more details about the told story elements, facilitating the telling of the story, showing a stance, displaying understanding or doubt, etc.. This section examines the responsive actions from story recipient that lead to side sequences.

4.3.1 Requesting details in the telling

In the dataset for this book, the most frequent recipient action that resulted in story suspension is a request for more details about the story told so far. Here, to request for more details describes a situation in which, targeting at certain told story elements, the story recipient asks for new and not given details.

Previous studies have found that requests for elaboration and clarification "contribute significantly to the shaping of the storyline" (Ochs & Capps, 2001, p. 31). Often, when a story recipient requests elaboration and clarification, the storyline may be adjusted accordingly to permit more details to be included in the story. When requesting and attending to the request becomes the focal business of the recipient and teller, the ongoing telling may be put on hold momentarily as the storyteller takes a turn to respond to the story recipient's request.

When a story recipient requests particular details, he/she is also making an attempt to establish and update her understanding of the story being told so far. Although the story recipient's request during the telling is responsive in nature (probing the story told so far), such requests often take a question format, and thus create a first pair part (henceforth FPP, Schegloff, 2007), which exerts great pressure on the storyteller to respond. An answer to the question becomes relevant or even obliged upon the occurrence of the story recipient's FPP question.

In (4-06), the ongoing telling is halted by the recipient's question about a detail in the story not mentioned by the teller. The extract is a reproduction of extract (4-04). Before the start of the extract, Li has been talking about the course her classmates took in university.

(4-06) ES_M04_0148_Department of Chinese [storyteller = Rui; recipient = Li]

01 芮 : e- 那 很 有意思 huh huh 昨天 我 还
Rui e- na hen youyisi huh huh zuotian wo hai
that very interesting yesterday I also

02 上网， 网 - 碰到 几个 中文系
shangwang wang-pengdao jige zhongwenxi
surf.the.net net meet several-CL department.of.Chinese

03 的 人 , = 然后 在网上 发 帖子 , =
de ren, = ranhou zaiwangshang fa tiezi,=
PRT person then on.the.Internet send post

04 [然后 -
[ranhou-
then
'That's very interesting, Yesterday, I also got on the Internet and met several people from the department of Chinese, and then (they) posted on the Internet, and then-'

05 李 : → [哪个 :: 学校 的 中文系 .=
Li [nage :: xuexiao de zhongwenxi.=
which-CL university PRT department.of.Chinese
'The department of Chinese at which university.'

06 芮 : = 应该 - (0.3) 不 知道 因为 网上 嘛 ,=
Rui =yinggai- (0.3) bu zhidao yinwei wangshang ma,=
should not know because on.the.Internet PRT

07 然后 他们 就 说 他们 [是 中文系， =
ranhou tamen jiu shuo tamen [shi zhongwenxi,=
then they just say they are department.of.Chinese
'Should-, I don't know, as it's on the Internet. They just said that they were from the department of Chinese,'

08 李： [>哦哦<]
Li [> o o <]
oh oh
'oh oh'

09 芮： =因为 他们 当年 学 了 什么， =
Rui =yinwei tamen dangnian xue le shenme,=
because they in.those.years learn ASP sth.like

10 中国 当代 文学 史 什么的，
zhongguo dangdai wenxue shi shenmede,
Chinese contemporary literature history and.the.like
'As they were studying something like History of Chinese Contemporary Literature,'

11 ((Rui returns to her story.))

As analyzed in Section 4.2, the story recipient Li's question in line 5 temporarily suspends the ongoing telling when the storyteller Rui turns to answer Li's inquiry.

By asking the question, 'The department of Chinese at which university' (line 5), Li shows her interest in a particular detail in the story. As Rui's characterization of the people she met on the internet as some people from a Chinese Department (lines 2 and 3), Li 'presses' a bit by an inquiry of the university to which the said Chinese Department is affiliated. Here, Li's inquiry takes the form of a typical question-word question (Li & Thompson, 1981) with the question word *nage* 'which' standing in the position of the asked-for information (line 5). In response to Li's inquiry, Rui admits that she actually does not know as those people just said they were from a Chinese department (lines 6-7). In this case, Li's inquiry is made at a point when Rui is recounting what those people did on the internet (line 3) and is obviously continuing along this line of telling when she says *ranhou* 'and then' (line 4). Li's request (line 5), on the other hand, is about a more specific detail in the description of the people being talked about in Rui's story. As such, it effects a suspension on the course of telling Rui is taking so far.

In (4-07), the story recipient also makes a request for details in a question format which makes a yes-or-no answer relevant. Prior to the extract, the storyteller, Jin, has been telling the other speaker, Yu, that in one episode of the TV show *Your Face Sounds Familiar*, the actress Qu Yin imitated rock star Cui Jian. The story is being told to back up Jin's opinion that the make-up artist on the show is very good at his job (line 2).

(4-07) SR_M17_0430_On-the-spot making up [storyteller = Jin; recipient = Yu]

01 瑾 : 然后 就 - 呃 我 觉得 - 那个 百变大咖秀 :,
Jin: ranhou jiu- e wo juede- nage baibiandakaxiu:,
then just uh I think that-CL Your.Face.Sounds.Familiar

02 他们 那个 [化妆师 真的 很 厉害 .
tamen nage [huazhuangshi zhende hen lihai.
their that-CL makeup.artist really very skillful
'And then- uh I think- that Your Face Sounds Familiar, their makeup artist is really very skillful.'

03 钰 : [mm
Yu: *[mm*

04 (0.8)

05 瑾 : 就 比如说 她 扮 崔健 嘛 ,= 鼻子 [这 要 :(.) =
Jin: jiu birushuo ta ban cuijian ma,= bizi [zhe yao:(.)=
then for.example she imitate NAME PRT nose here should

06 钰 : [mm
Yu: *[mm*

07 瑾 : = 可能 -, > 就是 那种 < 鼻 [子 不 是 这样 往下 =
Jin: = keneng-,> jiushi nazhong< bi [zi bu shi zheyang wangxia=
maybe that.is that-CL nose not be like.this downward

08 钰 : [他 -
Yu: [ta-
he
'He-'

09 瑾 : = 是 [往上的 嘛 .
Jin: = shi [wangshangde ma
be upward PRT
'For example, she impersonated Cui Jian,= the nose here shou:ld (.), maybe-, >that is that kind of< nose doesn't point downward like this, but upward.'

10 钰 : → [他 现场 化妆 的 吗 ?
Yu: [ta xianchang huazhuang de ma?
he on.the.spot makeup PRT Q
'Did he make her up on the spot?'

11 瑾: 对 呀, 他 就 现场 给 他们 画 呀, (.)
Jin: dui ya, ta jiu xianchang gei tamen hua ya, (.)
right PRT he just on.the.spot for they makeup PRT
'Yeah, he did makeup for them on the spot,'

12 然后 他们 还 叫 什么- [好莱坞 我 不 知道 是=
ranhou tamen hai jiao shenme- [haolaiwu wo bu zhidao shi=
then they also call sth. Hollywood I not know be

13 钰: [mm
Yu: *[mm*

14 瑾: =真的 假的.
Jin: =zhende jiade.
true false
'Right, he did the makeup for them on the spot, (.) and they were also called something Hollywood, I don't know whether that's true or not.'

15 ((Jin returns to the previously halted story.))

The extract begins with Jin's recounting of how the actress Qu Yin imitated a famous rock star Cui Jian (line 5) in a TV show, and Qu Yin needed to have her nose made up so that it would point upward instead of downward (lines 7 and 9). While Jin is constructing the utterance about the direction of the nose (lines 7 and 9), the story recipient Yu asks the question 'Did he do on-the-spot makeup?' (line 10), inquiring whether the make-up artist did the makeup for the actress Qu Yin on the spot in the TV show.

Here, a yes or no answer becomes relevant to Yu's question. Responding to this question (line 10), Jin provides the affirmative answer *dui a* 'right' (in line 11) and repeats *ta jiu xianchang gei tamen hua ya* 'he did makeup for them on the spot,' (line 11), implying that the task is very challenging and the make-up artist's skill is really good. Jin further adds that 'they are also called something Hollywood, I don't know whether that's true or not' (lines 12 and 14), before she returns to the halted telling. In this extract, upon the story recipient's request for details, the storyteller does not just provide a simple "yes" or "no" answer. Instead, more details (details not requested) are offered by the storyteller before she returns to the previous telling.

Extract (4-08) also shows a story recipient's request for more details. Here, instead of requesting more details of an element in the story, the recipient is concerned with something that is secondary to the storyline.

In this conversation, the storyteller Su recounts the boring tour they had in Singapore and complains about the bad arrangement made by the tour agency. Prior to this extract, Su has been telling Yi that the tour agency did not take the tourists to have local food in Singapore, but only let them have Chinese food.

(4-08) SR_M01_1518_Does cat eat watery things [storyteller = Su; recipient = Yi]

01 苏:　那些 中餐 啊 ,.h 好 :: [搞笑 就是 , (0.8) 就是 , =
Su:　naxie zhongcan a, .h hao::[gaoxiao jiushi, (0.8) jiushi,=
those Chinese.food PRT very funny that.is that.is

02 易:　[((咳嗽))((咳嗽))
Yi:　*[((cough))((cough))*

03 苏:　= 它 那个 xi- 那个 粥 : 很 稀 很 稀
Su:　= ta nage xi- nage zhou: hen xi hen xi
it that-CL that-CL porridge very watery very watery

04　很 稀 嘛 ,.h 稀 (h) 到 :(h) .h 最后 他们 就 - .h
hen xi ma,.h xi (h)dao:(h) .h zuihou tamen jiu- .h
very watery PRT watery-COMP finally they just

05　> 就是 < 有 一个 人 就是 , 其中 的 一个
>jiushi < you yige ren jiushi, qizhong de yige
that.is there.is one-CL person that.is among PRT one-CL

06　阿姨 就 说 , (0.3) 那 - 我们 那里 都 说 是 这 是
ayi jiu shuo,(0.3) na- women nali dou shuo shi zhe shi
auntie just say that we there all say be this be

07　喂 猫 :: 吃 的 那 (个 / 种) 猫 : 食 呢 (xx) 就是
wei mao:: chi de na (ge/zhong) mao:shi ne (xx) jiushi
feed cat eat PRT that(CL/type) cat.food PRT that.is

08　很 稀 很 稀 的 [嘛 .
hen xi hen xi de [ma.
very watery very watery PRT PRT
'That Chinese food,.h the funny thing was,(0.8)that is,= that porridge: was very very very watery,.h the porridge was so watery that.h finally one person, one of the aunties, said,(0.3) 'in our hometown people would say this is for cats, this is cat food.' (xx) That was very very watery.'

09 易: →　[猫 : 都 吃 稀 的 啊 .=
Yi:　[mao: dou chi xi de a.=
cat all eat watery PRT Q
'Do cats eat watery things.'

10 苏: =我 不 知(h)道(h), [他们 是 这样 形容 的, =
Su: = wo bu zhi(h) dao(h), [tamen shi zheyang xingrong de,=
I not know they be this-CL describe PRT
'=I don't know, they described it like this,='

11 易: [huh huh huh (.) huh .h
Yi: *[huh huh huh (.) huh .h*

12 苏: =.h 然后 反正 也 [不是 那么 很 好吃 啊 =
Su: =.h ranhou fanzheng ye [bushi name hen haochi a=
then anyway also not that very delicious PRT

13 易: [((咳嗽))
Yi: *[((cough))*

14 苏: =什么的 然后 后来,
Su: =shenmede ranhou houlai,
and.so.on then later
'=And anyway it didn't taste very good,'

15 ((Su returns to the halted story.))

The extract begins with Su's recounting that they had been served a Chinese breakfast (line 1) and that the porridge provided to them was very watery (lines 1-3). Then Su continues to report what one of the members in the group said about the porridge: 'in our hometown people would say this is for cats — it's cat food' (lines 4-7). When Su explains 'that is very very watery' (lines 7 and 8), Yi asks the question: 'Do cats eat watery things' (line 9).

To this Su responds, 'I don't know, they described it like this, and anyway it didn't taste very good' (lines 10, 12 and 14), which claims no knowledge of the answer to the question. She then explains that she is just reporting what other people said (line 10), and concludes the answer by saying 'anyway it didn't taste very good' (lines 12 and 14). Su then returns to her story sidetracked by Yi's question.

In this case, Su's telling centers on her complaint about the unsatisfactory meal arrangement of a tour group which is substantiated in her story of the watery porridge the group had for breakfast. Her complaint is upgraded when she reported a group member's comparison of the porridge to cat food, which is believed to be watery. In other words, cat food is not the main element in the telling but is mentioned as support to the complaint she is making. However, Su's reported comparison has caught the attention of Yi who asks the question on cat food which sidetracks from Su's telling. When Su turns to responds to Yi's question, the current focus of their talk also turns to the authenticity of the claimed quality of cat food within the side sequence.

The above three examples demonstrate how a story recipient's request for various details in the story being told so far interrupts the ongoing telling.

4.3.2 Facilitating the telling

Story recipients facilitate storytelling through collaboratively participating in the construction of the story. For instance, the story recipient may do an other-repair when the teller has produced an incorrect word and gets stuck in bringing their talk forward. They may also make a collaborative completion, or predict the storyline as ways to move the telling forward. However, as these actions from the recipient often make relevant a matching next action, e.g. granting a confirmation or rejection, the ongoing telling may be halted.

Other-repair is one of the repair types in which the recipient of a perceived trouble source in another speaker's turn provides a remedy to that trouble source (Schegloff, Jefferson and Sacks, 1977). The story recipient's initiation of other-repair may have the effect of halting the ongoing telling, as the storyteller responds by orienting to the recipient's repair. Following the "identical series" repair format identified by Jefferson (1987, p. 88), the occurrence of an other correction follows the sequence "X Y Y": in "X", "a speaker produces some object"; in the first "Y", "a subsequent speaker produces an alternative"; in the second "Y", "the prior speaker produces the alternative" (Jefferson, 1987, p. 88). In the context of a storytelling sequence, the "X" is an object or story element in the story told so far and the first "Y" is the other repair initiated by the story recipient. If the storyteller accepts the alternative produced by the story recipient (the first "Y"), the storyteller will also produce the same alternative (the second "Y").

Extract (4-09) is an example of how a story-recipient-initiated other-repair puts an ongoing telling on hold. This extract is a reproduction from extract (4-02). Recall that Lena's story is about the various sightseeing spots they visited during their trip to Beijing. The telling in (4-09) is about their visit to the historical site of the imperial mausoleums built by the emperors in the Ming Dynasty and known as the Thirteen Tombs.

(4-09) ES_M11_0513_Thirteen Tombs [storyteller = Lena; recipient = Tina]

01 LEN: 我们 当时 是 下午 四十 度 唉:, (.)
women dangshi shi xiawu sishi du ai:, (.)
we at.that.time be afternoon forty degree PRT

02 .h 我们 先 是 去 参观 那个:: (0.8) 十三: 水-
.h women xian shi qu canguan na-ge:: (0.8) shisan: shui-
we first be go visit that-CL thirteen water
'When we were there it was forty degrees in the afternoon, (.).h We first went to visit tha::t (0.8) Thirtee:n water-'

03 (.)

04 TIN: → 十三陵.=
shisanling.=
Thirteen.Tombs
'Thirteen Tombs.='

05 LEN: =哎-, 十三陵.=
= ai-, shisanling.=
INTJ Thirteen.Tombs
=*'Yeah-, Thirteen Tombs.'*=

06 TIN: =噢.
=ao.
INTJ
'=Ao.'

07 ((Lena returns to her story.))

As Lena starts to recount their visit to the tombs, she is apparently having problem in producing the place name and gets stuck at the term 'thirteen water' (line 2). It is at this point that Tina issues an other-repair by offering the correct term 'thirteen tombs' (line 4). By doing this, Tina is helping Lena to get on with her telling now that the correct place name is supplied for her. However, while Tina's other-repair may aim to help Lena to come out of a difficulty, it also makes relevant Lena's acceptance or rejection of the supplied form. The pattern of X, Y, Y can also be observed here – X being the incorrect 'thirteen water' produced by Lena, the first Y being the correct term 'thirteen tombs' supplied by Tina, and the second Y being the correct term repeated by Lena as acceptance of the correction. For the duration of the repair sequence both the teller and recipient focus on fixing a place reference. Although the telling sequence is briefly suspended by the repair sequence, the interactional work within the repair sequence nevertheless aims to move the course of telling forward by repairing a problem which has first hampered its progression. In this regard, Tina's other-repair is seen as facilitative in nature.

Next, I examine a case in which the side sequence is triggered by collaborative completion. The phenomenon of story recipient collaboratively completing the prior speaker's incomplete sentences with syntactically coherent parts was noticed by Sacks and articulated in his (1995a) lectures. Lerner (1991, 2004) also investigates collaborative completion (or pre-emptive completion) of the prior speaker's utterance by a subsequent speaker, stating that "pre-emptive completion is a bid to enter the ongoing turn of another speaker" (2004, p. 237). As Lerner observed, one position for a speaker to enter a prior speaker's talk is when the prior speaker is having difficulty in bring the TCU-in-progress to completion (Lerner, 1996). To supply talk as completing another's talk displays the supplier's understanding of both the content and format of the TCU-so-far, an understanding that makes relevant confirmation or rejection in the next turn by the prior speaker whose talk is being collaboratively completed. Therefore, recipient-produced collaborative completion and teller's response to it may form brief side sequence within the telling sequence.

In the next extract, (4-10), a story recipient's collaborative completion briefly puts the ongoing telling on hold. The storyteller, Ada, has been telling Bes that she and her friends were taught how to use computer software to create a 3D scene. Prior to this extract, Ada has just resumed her storytelling by recounting the procedures they used.

(4-10) SR_M18_2914_The sense of depth [storyteller = Ada; recipient = Bes]

01	Ada:	就是	(.)	导	张-	单张	图	嘛,=
		jiushi	(.)	dao	zhang-	danzhang	tu	ma,=
		that.is		export	CL	single	image	PRT
		'That is to export a- single image,'						
02	Bes:	= 啊						
		= a						
		ah						
		'Ah'						

03 Ada: (>把 它 <) 导 出来 然后 :, 做 完 景深[10]
(> ba ta<) dao chulai ranhou:, zuo wan jingshen
BA it export out then make finish depth.of.field

04 以后 再 放 进去 , .h 然后 它 就 那种 (0.3) Tch
yihou zai fang jinqu, .h ranhou ta jiu nazhong (0.3) Tch
after then put in then it just that-type

05 景深感 就 -
jingshengan jiu-
sense.of.depth just
'Export it and then, after making a larger depth of field, we put it in again, and it's sort of (0.3) Tch the sense of depth is just-'

06 (0.5)

07 Bes: → 更 [加强 .
geng [jiaqiang
more strengthened
'More strengthened.'

08 Ada: [很 强 很 强 了 .
[hen qiang hen qiang le.
very strong very strong PRT
'Very very strong.'

09 (0.8)

10 Ada: 对 .
dui
right
'Right.'

((Ada returns to her story.))

At the start of the extract Ada is describing the procedure of exporting a single image (line 1). She then continues to describe what they did after exporting it (line 3). When she begins to describe what happened 'after making a larger depth of field, we put it in again' (lines 3 and 4), she gets stuck as she tried to explain that 'the sense of depth is just-' (line 5). A 0.5-second pause ensues. Bes then produces a descriptive expression, 'more strengthened' (line 7), which is a syntactically coherent component to finish Ada's incomplete sentence, 'the sense of depth is just-' (line 5).

[10] Jingshen 'Oepth of field' is a technical term in photography.

The story recipient's collaborative completion, 'more strengthened' (line 7), produced upon Ada's apparent difficulty in completing her utterance, can be seen as responsive to this problem on Ada's side: Bes is trying to minimize the gap (line 6) by completing Ada's syntactically incomplete utterance (line 5) so that Ada can go on with the next bit in her story. As it turns out, just as Bes has started to produce 'more strengthened', Ada herself also picks up from where she got stuck by adding the phrase 'very very strong' (line 8). This shows that the item supplied by Bes is indeed on the same track as what Ada intends to say but is not able to do so a moment ago. As Bes' collaborative completion displays her understanding of what Ada meant to say, it makes Ada's confirmation or rejection a relevant next action. Although Ada's own 'very very strong' in a sense already confirms Bes' understanding, She nevertheless "officially" gives the confirmation with *dui* 'right' (line 10) after a noticeable gap (line 9) before she returns to her story. Ada's "delayed" start seems to suggest her orientation to the relevance or expectation of her response to Bes' collaborative completion. In this case, although the collaborative completion leads to the teller's response which for that brief moment orients to a matter separate from the story itself, it is nevertheless facilitative in nature similar to the other-repair seen in (4-09) above.

Sometimes a story recipient may also contribute to the development of a storyline by predicting what will happen next in the story. Recipient's predicting of what the teller possibly will tell next is a display of his/her close attention to the telling. Such prediction can be realized either in question or non-question format. Question-formatted predicting is similar to what Koike (2009) labels "guessing the next part of story": based on "information in the story-so-far as well as their prior general and personal knowledge" (p. 141) the story recipient predicts or guesses about the possible next happening. Non-question formatted predicting may sound more assertive. As prediction of what happened next in the story-so-far is to proffer a possible next bit in the course of telling, it makes confirmation, modification or reject as relevant next action on the part of the storyteller thus effecting a brief suspension of the ongoing telling. Extract (4-11) below is a case in point. The extract is a reproduction of 4-03 examined in Section 4.2.

As explained in Section 4.2, the storyteller Qi has been telling how her boyfriend was touched by the present she gave him, but she thinks that his present to her is not romantic at all.

(4-11) SR_M15_2505_Boyfriend [storyteller = Qi; recipient = Yue]

01 琪: 他 跟 我 送 什么, =一个 台灯, (.).h °我° 气 死 了.
Qi ta gen wo song shenme,= yige taideng, (.).h °wo° qi si le.
he with me send what one-CL lamp I mad die ASP

02 ((拍手)) (.) 他 还 说 挺 浪漫 的, 那天
((paishou)) (.) ta hai shuo ting langman de, natian
clap he even say pretty romantic PRT that.day

03 >寄过来< (.) 我 说 °嘶:° 你 给 我 买 什么, =>他 说<,=
>ji-guolai< (.) wo shuo °si:° ni gei wo mai shenme,=> ta shuo<
mail-COMP I say SOUND you for me buy what he say
'What did he send to me, = a lamp, (.).h This drove me mad. ((Clap))(.)He even told me on the day he mailed it to me that it was pretty romantic (.) I said '°si:° what did you buy for me,' =>he said<,='

04 悦: =(哦-)
Yue =(o-)
oh
'=(Oh-)'

05 (.)

06 琪: 因为- 我 告[诉 他:,
Qi yinwei- wo gao[su ta:,
because I tell him
'Because I told hi:m,'

07 悦: [mm
Yue *'[mm'*

08 悦: m[m
Yue *'m[m'*

09 琪: [我 虽然 这样 问 他, 你 千万别 告诉 我, 因为
Qi [wo suiran zheyang wen ta, ni qianwanbie gaosu wo, yinwei
I although this ask him you never tell me because

10 我 很 喜欢 追求 [惊喜.
wo hen xihuan zhuiqiu [jingxi.
I very like pursue surprise
'Although I asked him never to tell me what the present is, because I like the feeling of getting a surprise.'

11 悦: → [mm. 然后 他 告[诉 你 了.
Yue [mm. ranhou ta gao[su ni le.
then he tell you ASP
'mm. And then he told you.'

12	琪 : Qi		[他没 告诉 我 . [ta mei gaosu wo. he not tell me *'He didn't tell me.'*
13	悦 : Yue	哦 . o. oh *'Oh.'*	

((Qi returns to her story.))

As the analysis in Section 4.2 demonstrated, the story recipient Yue's prediction of what the story character 'her boyfriend' would do (line 11) sidetracks Qi's telling when the focus of their talk becomes ratifying if the prediction matches what is going to be told next. Here, Yue's prediction of what happens next in the story-so-far can be heard as an attempt to facilitate the ongoing telling in that her prediction is intended to move the story forward to the next bit in its course. Although Yue's declarative-formatted prediction (delivered with a falling intonation) 'And then he told you' (line 11) displays a relatively higher degree of certainty (compared to question-formatted prediction) on her part of what actually happened that Qi is going to tell next, it still needs to be confirmed by Qi in the next turn. As it turns out, the guess is incompatible to what Qi intends to tell next, and is rejected by her with the reply 'He didn't tell me' (line 12). This is then acknowledged by Yue in the next turn (line 13).

The three extracts examined in this section illustrate the ways that recipient actions which are intended to facilitate the progress of telling can nevertheless result in brief sidetrack. In the cases of recipient-produced other-repair and collaborative completion upon some difficulties in the teller's delivery of the story, and the prediction of the storyline at a dramatic point in the telling, the local focus of the talk deals with some aspects in the telling that makes relevant a response from the teller which is not part of the main telling.

4.3.3 Showing stance

As part of the telling sequence, the story recipient may offer an assessment, raise a different point of view, or even show his or her surprise, displaying a particular stance toward the story told so far. When the storyteller begins to orient to the recipient's showing of stance, the ongoing telling may again be interrupted.

It has been noticed that story recipients can make assessments in the middle of a multi-unit extended turn in storytelling (C. Goodwin, 1986). Goodwin explains that,

> "Even brief assessments can embody elaborated participation displays which permit recipient to react to the talk in progress by showing enthusiasm, appreciation, outrage, etc. and by positioning the assessment within the current unit speaker provides recipient a place for this display to run its course before proceeding to further talk" (p. 211).

During the telling sequence, the storyteller may occasionally pause and wait until the story recipient has finished his or her assessment before continuing the production of the next story unit (C. Goodwin, 1986). In this case, the storyteller does not take turn space to respond to the assessment offered by the story recipient. However, the storyteller may also orient to story recipient's assessment. Even if the turn space the storyteller takes to respond to the story recipient is minimal, a side sequence is occasioned once the storyteller begins to orient to the assessment.

Extract (4-12) below is an example in which the storyteller orients briefly to the story recipient's assessment during the telling sequence and then returns to her own telling. Prior to the extract, the storyteller Su has been telling Yi that the tour guide was unhappy with them because they did not buy the expensive jewelry. At line 1 Su is recounting her mother's opinion that the tour guide is very nice (line 1).

(4-12) SR_M01_1946_Like pupils [storyteller = Su; recipient = Yi]

01	苏 : Su	然后 后来 - 而且 我 妈 一直 觉得 很 好 ,= ranhou houlai-erqie wo ma yizhi juede hen hao,= then later and.also my mother always think very nice
02		你 > 知道 :< 好 到 - 她 : 觉得 什么 程度 吗 , .hh ni > zhidao:< hao dao- ta: juede shenme chengdu ma, .hh you know nice reach she think what degree Q
03		就是 如果 我 和 我 妈 讲 一句 话 , jiushi ruguo wo he wo ma jiang yiju hua, that.is if I and my mother say one-sentence utterance

04 =你 知道 我 妈 会 怎样 吗 .=
=ni zhidao wo ma hui zenyang ma.=
you know my mother would how Q
'And then later my mother kept thinking that (the tour guide) was very nice, = you know, she thinks (the tour guide) was so nice that, if I said something to my mother, = you know what my mother would do.'

05 易 : =mm
Yi =mm

06 苏 : ° 嘿 h 别 讲话 , 导游 在 讲话 , = 认真 听 .°=
Su °hei h bie jianghua, daoyou zai jianghua,= renzhen ting.°
hey not speak tour.guide is speaking carefully listen
'Hey, don't speak, the tour guide is speaking, listen carefully.'

07 易 : =.hhh (.) 哦 ::[:::::: hoh
Yi =.hhh (.) O ::[:::::: hoh

08 苏 : [你 知道 吗? 就是 到 那种 程度 ,=
Su [ni zhidao ma? jiushi dao nazhong chengdu,
you know Q that.is reach that-type degree

09 因为 她 觉得 那个 导游 那么 好 应该
yinwei ta juede nage daoyou name hao yinggai
because she think that-CL tour.guide so nice should

10 尊重 [她 那种 感觉 的 .
zunzhong [ta nazhong ganjue de.
respect her that-type feeling PRT
'You know what? It's that degree, because she thinks the tour guide is very nice and (we) should respect her, that kind of feeling.'

11 易 : → [好像 小学生 哦 .
Yi [haoxiang xiaoxuesheng o.
like pupil.in.primary.school PRT
'Like pupils in primary school.'

12 苏 : 对 啊 .
Su dui a
right PRT
'Right.'

((Su returns to her story.))

Su continues to tell Yi that her mother respects the tour guide so much that when Su tried to talk with her mother, her mother would stop her and ask Su to listen to the tour guide carefully (lines 2-4, 6, and 8-10). When Su is explaining the reason behind her mother's positive, respectful opinion of the tour guide (lines 9 and 10), Yi makes an evaluative remark, 'Like pupils in primary school' (line 11), comparing the behaviour of Su's mother's to that of pupils in primary school who usually listen to teachers very carefully.

This assessment is responded to by Su with an agreement token *dui a* 'right' (line 12) before she continues with her telling. Yi's assessment shows her monitoring of the story in progress, and her stance on a particular component in the story-so-far. It also creates an opportunity for the storyteller's response in the next turn. When the storyteller does take up the opportunity for a follow-up assessment, a minimal side sequence then comes into being during which the local focus of the talk sidetracks from the progression of the main telling as the storyteller orients to the evaluative action of the recipient. In the current case, as Su responds to Yi's assessment with a minimal agreement token, the assessment sequence is brief and does not halt the main telling for long as Su returns to her story in the TCU next to the agreement token.

In the next example, a dissenting view offered by the story recipient towards a particular element in the story-so-far halts the ongoing telling. The extract, (4-13), is taken from a conversation where three girls are chatting while also eating snacks and fruits. Before the start of the extract, Lin was offering some mangosteen fruit to the other two girls, Fen and Wan. On seeing Wan's refusal of the offer, Lin upgraded the offer by making a positive assessment about the fruit, and launched a story about the fruit. Line 1 of the extract is where Lin begins to recount her trip to Malaysia with her mother and how she persuaded her mother to eat the mangosteen (lines 1-3).

(4-13) SR_M09_0605_Mangosteen [storyteller = Lin; recipient = Fen and Wan]

01	琳： Lin:	那个 时候，(.) 我们 去 马来西亚 的 时候，(.) 我 妈 nage shihou, (.) women qu malaixiya de shihou, (.) wo ma that-CL time we go Malaysia PRT time my mother
02		就 - 她 - 我 就 很 喜欢 吃 我 就 说 啊 :: jiu- ta- wo jiu hen xihuan chi wo jiu shuo a:: just she I just very like eat I then say INT
03		我们 吃 这个 吧 ,(.) 然后 我 妈 就 - 看 这个 women chi zhege ba, (.) ranhou wo ma jiu- kan zhege we eat this-CL PRT then my mother just look this-CL

04			样子　就　觉得 不 好吃　　嘛 .= yangzi jiu juede bu haochi ma.= look just think not delicious PRT *'When my mother and I went to Malaysia, (.) my mother- just- she- I really like it and then I said, 'Ah:: let's have it',(.)and then my mother felt its taste wouldn't be good as she looked at the appearance of the fruit.='*
05	芬 : Fen:	→	=超　好吃　　的 .= =chao haochi de.= super delicious PRT *'=It's super delicious.='*
06	琳 : Lin:		= 对　啊　我 觉得 好　好吃　　的 . = dui a wo juede hao haochi de. right PRT I think very delicious PRT *'Right, I think it's very delicious.'*
07			((The side sequence becomes more elaborated.))

Lin is telling that because she herself liked the fruit so she suggested her mother to eat the fruit. Next, Lin reports that her mother did not feel the fruit would be tasty upon seeing what the fruit looks like (lines 3 and 4). To this reported negative feeling of the fruit by Lin's mother one of the story recipients Fen protests, 'It's super delicious' (line 5), displaying her strong disagreement towards the mother's feeling about the mangosteen. Fen's assessment is delivered at a point when Lin's story is still in progress, but Fen is quick to come in and display her stance towards a particular element in the story-so-far, i.e. the taste of mangosteen. Then Lin shows her agreement in the next turn where she says 'Right, I think it's very delicious' (line 6). As can be seen, Fen's stance towards the negative assessment of a fruit reported in the telling is a strong one (as evidenced by her choice of the adverb 'super') and it triggers a side sequence where Lin's ongoing telling gives way to the affiliation she expresses towards Fen's stance.

The story recipient may also show surprise to a particular element in the story told so far. As such stance display creates space for storyteller's response in the next turn, the ongoing telling may be momentarily put on hold as the teller responds to the recipient's stance display, as analyzed in (4-12) and (4-13) above. Extract (4-14) is another example. Here, the story recipient's show of surprise also sidetracks the ongoing telling. Prior to the extract, Liu has asked Ren what kind of exercise Ren does besides swimming. The extract begins with Ren's response to Liu's question.

(4-14) SR_M19_1108_Belly dance [storyteller = Ren; recipient = Liu]

01 任 : 我 以前 在 学校 的 时候 有 去 健身房
Ren: wo yiqian zai xuexiao de shihou you qu jianshenfang
I previously at school PRT time have go gym.room

02 办 过 卡 :, 但是 那个 条件 就 . hhh
ban guo ka:, danshi nage tiaojian jiu. hhh
register ASP membership but that-CL environment just

03 坚持 了 一个 月 的 跳 那个 肚皮舞 跟
jianchi le yige yue de tiao nage dupiwu gen
keep ASP one-CL month PRT dance that-CL belly.dance and

04 拉丁 还有 ::
lading haiyou::
Latin and
'When I was at school, I went to the gym room and registered for a membership, but their environment was just .hhh I went there for one month and had belly dance and Latin and::'

05 (.)

06 刘 : → ° 噢° , 你 还 [会 跳 肚皮舞 :?
Liu: ° ao° , ni hai [hui tiao dupiwu:?
ao you also can dance belly.dance
'Ao, you can also do belly dance?'

07 任 : [健身房 那些 < 器 : 材 >.
Ren: [jianshenfang naxie <qi:cai>.
gym.room those equipment
'Those equipment in the gym room.'

08 (.)

09 任 : [> 也< 就 学 了 嘛 , 学 了 一 [点点 , 就 跟着 =
Ren: [> ye< jiu xue le ma, xue le yi [diandian, jiu genzhe=
just learn ASP PRT learn ASP a.bit just follow

10 刘 : [huh [噢
Liu: [huh [Ao

11 = 别人 去 跳 [.h 主要 是 报 的 拉丁舞 班 .
=bieren qu tiao[.h zhuyao shi bao de ladingwu ban.
others go dance mainly be register PRT Latin.dance course
'I just learned, learned a little bit, just followed others to dance. .h The main thing was the Latin dance course I registered in.'

12 ((Ren returns to her story.))

In Ren's answer, she recounts her experience in taking part in exercise classes in a gym room for one month, where she learned belly dance and Latin dance (lines 1-4). It is clear that at line 4 Ren is obviously showing she has more to add to the list of exercises she did in the gym when she says *haiyou::* 'and' (line 4). However, it seems that she is searching for the next item when she stretches the second syllable of *haiyou*:: 'and' followed by a brief pause. It is at this point that the story recipient Liu asks a question on an item just mentioned in the telling so far, 'Ao, you can also do belly dance?' (line 6), displaying Liu's surprise at what Ren learned to do from taking classes in the gym⑪.

As it turns out, just a little after Liu has started to produce the utterance in line 6 that shows her surprise, Ren is able to pick up from *haiyou* 'and' (line 4) to tell that she also used other fitness equipment in the gym (line 7). This last item on her reported list of exercises is produced in overlap with Liu's display of surprise on the first item in her list (i.e. belly dance). However, it is clear that Ren has heard Liu despite their overlapping talk as evidenced in her response started from line 9. While Liu's question at line 6 can be heard as displaying her stance on Ren being able to do belly dance as something remarkable, Ren's response seems to be a play-down as she explained that she just learned a little bit of the belly dance. Note that Ren actually has the opportunity to continue her story as the completion point of her listing of the gym activities (line 7) has come out of the overlap with Liu's stance display (line 6). Should she continue from there by moving her telling forward with the next TCU, as she is entitled to as the storyteller, the import of Liu's stance display would be sequentially deleted without Ren's uptake. But as it turns out, Ren chooses to put her story on hold until she responds to Liu's surprise. In this case, Ren may be interactionally motivated to respond to Liu's stance display at the expense of being sidetracked. She may run the risk of being seen as agreeing with Liu that she herself also takes her being able to do belly dance as something remarkable should she choose not to respond to Liu.

The extracts examined in this section show that recipient evaluative actions often make the storyteller's affiliative/disaffiliative action as a relevant next. And as

---

⑪ Belly dance is not a very popular item in comparison to Latin dance as a common everyday exercise in gyms.

the storyteller produces these relevant actions, the telling of their own story would be temporarily put on hold.

4.3.4 Displaying understanding

The telling sequence may also be temporarily put on hold when the story recipient's understanding display of the story told so far is responded to by the storyteller at the expense of momentary sidetrack from the storyline. The story recipient's understanding can be shown in various ways, such as reformulating the story, providing additional information, initiating another storytelling sequence, etc.

The first example, (4-15), shows a story recipient reformulating what has been told in the story. The story recipient here uses a brief reformulation to show her understanding of a particular element in the story-so-far. Prior to the extract, the storyteller Rui has been recounting what the students did to fulfill a course she also took. Rui has told Li that the teaching assistant for the course would invite students to have dinner at the university restaurant if they actively participated in the discussion forum on the Internet. The extract begins with Rui's recounting of how she and her classmates were treated to dinner by the teaching assistant and had a very long, free chat when eating together (lines 1-4).

(4-15) ES_M04_0715_Having dinner [storyteller = Rui; recipient = Li]

01	芮: Rui	我 还 去 了 一次 然后 - 弄 了 一桌菜, wo hai qu le yici ranhou- nong le yizhuocai, I also go ASP once then make ASP one-table-dish
02		= 然后 (xx)(.)> 大家 -< 然后 大家就 开始 > 都 < = ranhou(xx)(.)> dajia-< ranhou dajia jiu kaishi > dou< then all then all just begin all
03		畅谈, = 然后 闲扯 :, .h 然后 会 - 会 讲 changtan, = ranhou xianche:,.h ranhou hui- hui jiang talk.freely then chat then will will talk
04		很 长 时间, .h 然后 (xxx-) 然后 就 - (0.3) hen chang shijian, .h ranhou (xxx-) ranhou jiu - (0.3) very long time then then just
05		但 - 只要 你 参加 过 那 以后 基本上 就是 dan- zhiyao ni canjia guo na yihou jibenshang jiushi but only you join ASP that after basically that.is

06 那 课堂 讨论 分 他会-都会 给 你 了,
na ketang taolun fen ta hui-dou hui gei ni le,
that class discussion mark he will all will give you PRT

07 .h 然[后- 嗯:
.h ran [hou- en:
then
'I also went there once and he (the teaching assistant) ordered lots of food, = and then all the people began to talk and chat freely for a long time, .h and (xxx) and as long as you joined that dinner, basically, he would give you the marks for class discussion, .h and then- en:'

08 李: → [参加 过 吃饭 就 给 [° 分° . (.) [huh huh
Li [canjia guo chifan jiu gei [° fen° . (.) [huh huh
join ASP have.dinner just give mark
'He gave you marks after you joined the dinner. Huh huh'

09 芮: [对 对 (x-) [因为
Rui [dui dui (X-)[yinwei
right right because

10 你 要 先 在 论坛 上 (.) 灌很多水
ni yao xian zai luntan shang (.) guanhenduoshui
you need first in forum in send.many.posts

11 他才 会 请 你 [去 . huh
ta cai hui qing ni [qu. huh
he only will invite you go
'Right, right (x-) because you had to send many posts to the forum. He would only invite you after that. huh'

12 李: [哦 :::::?=
Li [o:::::?=
oh
'Oh::::::?='

((Rui returns to her previously halted telling and continues to tell the story.))

Then Rui continues to tell Li that 'as long as you joined the dinner basically he would give you the marks for class discussion' (lines 5 and 6). As Rui is continuing her story — indicated by *ranhou* 'and then' in line 7 — Li produces the utterance 'He gave you marks after you joined dinner. Huh huh' (line 8), reformulating what has been told so far. Li's reformulation is constructed in such a way that it displays her understanding of the main point in the story-so-far, i.e. students get marks for joining the dinner with the teaching assistant.

In response to Li's reformulation, Rui says, 'Right, right, because you had to send many posts to the forum; he would only invite you after that. huh' (lines 9-11). She first confirms Li's reformulation (it is indeed the case that students would get marks after joining the dinner). Then she explains that this is so because the students have already met the requirement of active participation in posting discussion on the internet forum before becoming eligible to be invited to the dinner. The reformulation proffers a particular understanding of the story-so-far; the turn following it where the storyteller may display their checking on whether the reformulation-formatted understanding matches what he/she intended to convey. As shown in (4-15), this is what happens at lines 8-12 where Li's understanding display triggers a three-turn side sequence during which Rui's story is temporarily suspended.

A story recipient may also display their understanding of a particular element mentioned in the story-so-far by supplying "items" from their own independent epistemic domain. When a story recipient does this, the progression of the story may also temporarily give way to the new focus of the moment which deals with recipient understanding display.

Let us examine extract (4-05) again, reproduced as (4-16) below. Recall that in this part of the conversation Lena is recounting her holiday in Beijing with her family and friend where they visited a number of places. At the start of the extract, Lena's telling is about their visit to two adjacently placed historical sites: the Forbidden City and the imperial garden now called Jingshan Park. Lena starts by telling Ruth that they spent three hours in the Forbidden City, but then turns to describe the route of their visit, i.e. they actually visited the park first (lines 1-3, 6, 8).

(4-16) ES_M11_0553_Jing Shan Park [storyteller = Lena; recipient = Ruth]

01	Len:	故宫 我们 玩 了 三个 小时 大概. gugong women wan le sange xiaoshi dagai. Forbidden.City we visit PRT three-CL hour about
02		[(0.6)[我们 是 从 后门 往 前门 走 的. [(0.6)[women shi cong houmen wang qianmen zou de. we be from back.door toward front.door walk PRT *'We stayed in the Forbidden City for about three hours.* *(0.6) We walked from the back door to the front door.'*

03	Rut:		[.h [故 - [.h [gu- *'.h Gu-'*
04			(0.6)
05	Rut:		哦 ::[:, o ::[:,
06	Len:		[我们 先 去 的 那个 景山 嘛 . [women xian qu de nage jingshan ma. we first go PRT that-CL Jing.Shan PRT *'We first went to Jing Shan.'*
07	Rut:		.h 噢 对 .= .h ao dui.= INTJ right *'.h Ao right.='*
08	Len:		=.h 景山 然后 [翻过去 的 . =.h jingshan ranhou [fanguoqu de. Jing.Shan then climb.over PRT *'=.h Jing Shan and then we climbed over it.'*
09	Rut:	→	[那个 -(.) 皇帝 的 后花 [园 . [nage- (.) huangdi de houhua[yuan that-CL emperor PRT private.garden *'That- the emperor's private garden.'*
10	Len:		[对 对 对 [dui dui dui right right right *'Right right right'*
11			((Lena returns to her story.))

As analyzed in Section 4.2, Lena's story gets halted when Ruth comes in to say: 'That- the Emperor's private garden' (line 9). This place reference to the same park mentioned in Lena's story-so-far displays Ruth's knowledge of the history of the park independent of Lena's telling. That is, the history of the park is knowledge within Ruth's own epistemic domain. By providing an alternative reference to the park, Ruth displays her close attention to the telling and her understanding of which place is being talked about. As an understanding display, the proffered place reference out of the recipient's own epistemic domain is also subject to the teller's endorsement. In the case under examination, Lena is quick to confirm the alternative place reference (as evidenced in her early start at line 10) when she enthusiastically responds with a succession of three *dui dui dui* 'right, right, right' (line 10). The enthusiasm in her delivery of the confirmation could be heard as conveying an additional message that the history of the park is in her epistemic domain as well (Heritage & Raymond, 2005).

A further way of displaying understanding to a current story is recipient's producing of his/her own story. Sacks (1995a) notes that, "in hearing what another person says, one is reminded of one's own experience" and "such experiences are the analysis of whatever they say yields" (p.769)[12]. It is also not uncommon to find that a story recipient responds to a storytelling with a second story which "very nicely picks up the point of the first" (Sacks, 1995a, p. 767). In the data collection being examined for this research, it is found that the recipient is not limited to producing a second story upon the completion of the current story. They sometimes offer their own experience in a multi-unit turn which may potentially derail the current story-in-progress. As this kind of recipient action is observed within an ongoing story, it falls within the scope of the present research. Here, I prefer to use the phrase 'initiating the story recipient's own experience' (but not 'a second story'), because the "interruptive" telling of one's own experience may not develop into a full-fledged storytelling sequence.

In (4-17), the story recipient initiates a telling of her own experience in playing a game similar to the one just described by the storyteller. Prior to the extract, the storyteller Su has been telling Yi that she visited Universal Studios in the United States and played a game called "The Simpsons Ride" which used a stunning 3D effect that made people feel like they were entering the real world of the Simpsons. Su has been recounting her experience of riding on a roller coaster in that game. At the start of the extract, Su is telling about her feeling when riding on the roller coaster, when all of the people on the ride fell down suddenly (lines 1 and 2).

(4-17) SR_M01_0731_The Simpsons Ride [storyteller = Su; recipient = Yi]

01	苏：	我们：就 感觉 wong:: 一下 >我们 <就 全部
	Su:	women: jiu ganjue wong:: yixia >women< jiu quanbu
		we just feel ONO once we just all

[12] Sacks (1995b, p. 442) also identifies one rule for listening to stories: 'listen to a story to find out if a similar thing or the same thing happened to you. At the end of the story, if you've found such a thing, tell it.'

02			下[去 了 那种，.h 然后 还 有 什么， ((sniff))= xia[qu le nazhong,.h ranhou hai you shenme, go.down ASP that-kind then also have something ((sniff)) *'We just felt wong:: we all went down, and then there was something, ((sniff))='*
03	易： Yi:		[哦:::， [o:::, oh *'Oh:::,'*
04	苏： Su:		=呃-被 那些 东西 ::怎么 怎么样， =然后 你 这里 =e- bei naxie dongxi:: zenme zenmeyang,=ranhou ni zheli uh BEI those thing how how then you here
05			就 抖来抖去 抖来抖去，=其实 你 就 只是 在 jiu doulaidouqu doulaidouqu,= qishi ni jiu zhishi zai just keep.shaking keep.shaking actually you just only in
06			一个 比 这个 房子 还要 小 的 一个 地方， yige bi zhege fangzi haiyao xiao de yige difang, one-CL BI this-CL room even small PRT one-CL place
07			=一个 黑黑 的 [房子 里面. =yige heihei de [fangzi limian. one-CL dark PRT room inside *'=Uh- we were (shaked) by those things, =and then you kept shaking, =but actually you were just in a room that was smaller than this room, in the dark.'*
08	易： Yi:	→	[噢::，我 知道 了，我 [以前 坐= [ao::, wo zhidao le, wo [yiqian zuo= ao I know PRT I used.to sit *'Ao::, I got it, I used to sit='*
09	苏： Su:		[嗯:: [en:: en *'En::'*
10	易： Yi:		=过 有点： 像 那种 太空船， 然后 它 就 =guo youdian: xiang nazhong taikongchuan, ranhou ta jiu ASP a.bit like that-kind spacecraft then it just
11			四周 都 是 那种 (.)屏幕， 然后 你 就 sizhou dou shi nazhong (.) pingmu, ranhou ni jiu all.around all be that-kind screen then you just

12 看 超 漂亮 的 感觉.
kan chao piaoliang de ganjue.
watch super beautiful PRT feeling
'=It seemed like some kind of spacecraft, and then it just had this kind of screen all around, and it looked super beautiful when you watched it.'

Su continues to describe the physical experience of that game, such as being shaken all the time (lines 4 and 5), and mentions that the room they stayed in was actually a very small dark room (lines 5-7). When Su is constructing the utterance 'in a dark room' (line 7), the story recipient Yi utters a realization token 'Ao::' which prefaces *wo zhidao le* 'I got it' (line 8) and the ensuing telling of her own experience with riding the spaceship in the amusement park 'I used to sit =it seemed like some kind of spaceship, and then it just had this kind of screen all around, and it looked super beautiful when you watched it' (lines 8, 10-12).

By describing a similar experience, i.e. an exciting ride in stunning virtual space created by 3D technology, Yi displays an emphatic understanding of the kind of exciting feeling Su is trying to describe in her story of taking the Simpsons Ride.

This section examines recipient's action which displays their understanding of some elements in the story-so-far in relation to the progression of the telling. The extracts examined provide some samples of the ways their understanding of the ongoing story may be displayed. Through reformulation the story recipient can show their grasp of the high point in the story-so-far. Provision of an alternative reference term is also a means to show the recipient's understanding of the place being talked about in the story. Offering one's own feeling of a similar experience is another way that recipient makes use of to display their understanding of the storyteller's feeling about the experience being told in the story. As what recipient offers is a possible understanding on their part, the storyteller's endorsement is made relevant as the next action, and this often results in temporary suspension of the storyline itself.

4.4 Expanded side sequence

When a side sequence is occasioned by story recipient's response, it may get further elaborated and expanded. On some occasions, contingencies may arise in the course of the side sequence so the story teller may not immediately return to the suspended telling as he/she deals with that contingency first thus expanding the side sequence. On other occasions, a side sequence may be expanded as a result of 'sequence design' when the side-sequence initiating turn by the recipient is designed to subsequently introduce more substantial talk by himself. In addition to story recipient's response, the data shows that the storyteller may also expand the side sequence and it may develop into a more complex side sequence.

4.4.1 Side sequence expanded due to emergent contingencies

First, the side sequence may be expanded because of story recipient's follow-up questions. These questions may be used to request for clarification for what has not been clearly explained from the story recipient's perspective. These questions may also be used to request for other relevant details about the story told so far.

The following two examples illustrate two different contingencies during the side sequence leading to the expansion of the current side sequence.

Prior to (4-18), Su was telling what had happened in a jewelry shop on her trip. The tourists, including her, were brought to the shop by the tour guide who appeared very unhappy with them when they did not buy anything in that shop.

(4-18) SR_M01_1840_Medicinal Oil [storyteller = Su; recipient = Yi]

01	苏：	然后 她 就：(.) 而且 她 - 她 也 - 她：反正 就 (说)
	Su:	ranhou ta jiu: (.) erqie ta- ta ye- ta: fanzheng jiu(shuo)
		then she just also she she also she anyway that.is
02		心里 已经 有点 不爽， [.hh 然后 她 (ju-) 又 =
		xinli yijing youdian bushuang,[.hh ranhou ta(ju-) you =
		in.mind already a.bit not.happy then she again
03	易：	[mm
	Yi:	*[mm*
04	苏：	= 带 我们 去 什么 药油 店 啊 什么 店
	Su:	= dai women qu shenme yaoyou dian a shenme dian
		bring us go what medicinal.oil shop PRT what shop
05		[> 然后 <
		[>ranhou<
		then
		'Then she also felt unhappy with us anyway, and went on bringing us to shops like medicinal *oil shop and then'*

06	易 : Yi:	→	[药 什 [么 ↑ 店 [yao shen[me ↑ dian medicine what shop *'What kind of drugstore'*
07	苏 : Su:		[就 - (.) 药油 . [jiu- (.) yaoyou. it.is medicinal.oil *'It's medicinal oil.'*
08			(.)
09	苏 : Su:		[就 新加坡 药油 :: 很 出名 . [jiu Xinjiapo yaoyou hen chuming. just Singapore medicinal.oil very famous *'Singapore is very famous for its medicinal oil.'*
10	易 : Yi:	→	[°> 什么 叫< 药油 °. [°> shenme jiao< yaoyou°. what name medicinal.oil *'What is medicinal oil.'*
11			(.)
12	苏 : Su:		[就是 - (.) 卖 药 的 那些 . [jiushi- (.) mai yao de naxie. that.is sell medicine PRT those *'That is those shops where people sell medicine.'*
13	易 : Yi:	→	[什么 东西 啊 . [shenme dongxi a. what thing PRT *'What's that.'*
14			(0.3)
15	易 : Yi:	→	油 是 什么 [° 油 °. you shi shenme [°you°. oil is what oil *'What kind of oil is it.'*
16	苏 : Su:		[油 就是 :: (0.6) 喝 >的 那个< 油 :. [you jiushi:: (0.6) he >de nage< you:. oil that.is drink PRT that-CL oil *'Oil is the oil that you can drink.'*
17			((Su continues to explicate what kind of oil the medicated oil is and its functions, and the story recipient also joins to discuss the oil with the storyteller. After Yi finally shows her understanding, Su returns to her suspended story and recounted that actually they bought something in those shops.))

At the start of (4-18) Su is continuing with the story of their shopping experience and told Yi that they were then brought to a shop selling medicinal oil (lines 1, 2, and 4). At this point Su is obviously continuing when she says *ranhou* 'then' at line 5. However, this is overlapped by Yi's other-initiation on the kind of shop they were brought to ('What kind of drugstore' at line 6). Apparently, Yi is having trouble with the second syllable of the word *yaoyoudian* (literally: medicine oil shop) when Su mentions it in line 4 as manifested in the format of her other-initiation *yao shenme dian* (literally: medicine what shop). As other-initiation makes relevant self-repair by the trouble-source speaker in the next turn, Su, who has already withdrawn from her telling due to the overlapping other-initiation by Yi, now self-repairs by repeating *yaoyou* 'medicinal oil' (line 7). Here, Yi's other-initiation occasions a side sequence which suspends the progression of Su's telling about what happened in the medicinal oil shop. During the two turns at lines 6-7 the focal 'business' is on repairing a trouble source in Su's telling. As exemplified in Section 4.3.2, the completion of self-repair is a locus where the side sequence can be closed if the storyteller returns to the main telling in the next TCU (table 1). Or the sequence-closing third may be produced by the other-initiation speaker after which another locus is provided for the teller to go back to the suspended course of telling thus closing the side sequence. However this is not what happens in the case being examined here. It turns out that the side sequence gets expanded after a brief gap (line 8) where Yi issues a second other-initiation at line 10 (in overlap with Su's line 9 where she seems to be dealing with the brief gap at line 8 by adding further talk about the medicinal oil). Yi's second other-initiation *shenme jiao yaoyou a* 'what is medicinal oil' shows he has heard the second syllable in *yaoyou* (medicinal oil) in Su's self-repair but a new trouble source arises for her as to what medicinal oil is. When seeing no immediate self-repair from Su (as evidenced by the brief pause in line 11), Yi follows up with a further other-initiation at line 13 *shenme dongxi* a 'what is that'. With these other-initiations from Yi, the side sequence remains open. Then after a 0.3-second pause (line 14), Yi launches the fourth other-initiation *shenme you a* 'What oil is it' (line 15). It can be seen in this case that a first other-initiation by the story recipient leads to the start of a side sequence in which more other-initiations are launched either because the responding self-repair creates new trouble source or it fails to solve the trouble source targeted by the other-initiation. In other words, the expansion of the side sequence in (4-18) is contingent on storyteller's problematic responses to story recipient's other-initiation.

When the requested repairing work is not sufficiently and exactly provided by the storyteller, the side sequence gets further expanded because of the recipient's follow-up other-initiations.

Extracts (4-19) below is a case with an expanded side sequence resulting from a series of recipient's questions targeting at a number of aspect in the story being told so far.

The participants, Liang and Chen, in (4-19) are postgraduate students in the same department. Prior to the extract, they have been talking about a coordinator who organized activities and made a newsletter for their department. Liang has told Chen that she received newsletters from her former school every year. And at the beginning of (4-19), she tells Chen that she has given the newsletter she received to that coordinator for his reference (lines 1, 2 and 4).

(4-19) ES_M01_0453_Newsletter [storyteller = Liang; recipient = Chen]

01	梁 : Liang	我 就 ::: 把 -(0.3) 我 就 把 : 那个 .hh 呃 : 我们 wo jiu ::: ba- (0.3) wo jiu ba: nage .hh e: women I just BA I just BA that-CL uh our
02		学校 寄 给 我 的 newslet[ter,(.) 呃 : 给 他 :::= xuexiao ji gei wo de (.) e: gei ta:::= school send to me PRT newslet[ter uh to him
03	陈 : Chen	[mm mm [mm mm
04	梁 : Liang	= 拿 了 一份儿 [让 他 作 ce-(.) 参考 咯 .= = na le yifen'er [rang ta zuo ce-(.) cankao lo.= take ASP one.copy let him as reference PRT *'I just sent him one copy of the newsletter my school sent to me, and let him take it as a reference.'*
05	陈 : Chen	[mm *[mm*
06	陈 : Chen	=mm mm= =mm mm=
07	梁 : Liang	=mm(.)[我 没有 .h(.) 就是 :: 没有 具 < 体 > 跟 他 = =mm(.)[wo meiyou .h(.) jiushi:: meiyou ju <ti> gen ta= mm I not that.is not particularly with him

```
08    陈:                  [哦
      Chen                 [O

09    梁:            =讲   [(.)(yue:)  ((清嗓子))
      Liang          =jiang [(.)(yue:) ((qingsangzi))
                      say               clear.throat
                     'mm (.) I didn't (.) I mean I didn't particularly tell him (.) (yue:)'

10    陈:    →            [是:也 是 用 英文 做 的 吗.=
      Chen                [shi: ye shi yong yingwen zuo de ma.=
                           be also be use English make PRT Q
                          'Is: is it also in English.'

11    梁:            =是 啊, 是 [啊,
      Liang          = shi a, shi [a,
                       yes PRT yes PRT
                      'Yes, yes,'

12    陈:    →                       [mm:(.) 是:: 就说 是 他们 :::.hh(.) 嗯 :::
      Chen                           [mm:(.) shi:: jiushuo shi tamen:::.hh(.) en:::
                                      mm be that.is be they en

13                   你们 原来 的 faculty:: [还是::
                     nimen yuanlai de         [haishi::
                     you former PRT faculty    or
                     'mm (.) Is it their::: en::: your former faculty or:::'

14    梁:                                      [对 对 - faculty 的.
      Liang                                    [dui dui- de.
                                                right right faculty PRT
                                               'Right right- faculty's.'

15                   ((Chen continues to ask question about who made the newsletter and who the
                     targeted readers were.))
```

When Liang is still constructing the TCU which projects a telling about what she had not mentioned to that coordinator when she gave him the newsletter (lines 7 and 9), Chen launches a question about the language in which the newsletter was published 'Is: is it also in English' (line 10). Chen's question at this point can be taken as 'interruptive' as it intercepts a TCU-in-progress in the course of Liang's telling. As Liang turns to give an answer to Chen's question, both the progression of her current TCU and the telling for which the TCU is a part is put on hold. As soon as Liang confirms that the newsletter was written in English (line 11), Chen is quick to launch another question 'is it their::: en::: your former faculty or:::' (lines 12 and 13) which seeks information of another detail about the newsletter - the people involved in producing that newsletter. Chen's follow-up question thus further expands the occasioned side sequence. In this case, the expanded side sequence results from the recipient asking more than one question about details of various aspects in the story being told so far.

Other forms of contingencies may also emerge. The following two examples show that when the story recipients tend to orient to the emergence of contingencies during the side sequence, it will develop into a further expanded one.

Prior to this extract, (4-20), the storyteller Su has been telling Yi about her mom's trip to Singapore. As she was also in Singapore at that time, she wanted to take the opportunity to see her mom and hoped to be able to do so by joining her mom's tour group for the local sightseeing. She has been complaining to Yi about the tour guide who did not like Su's request to join their tour for a day when she called her about the matter. At the start of the extract, Su is recounting her telephone conversation with the tour guide.

(4-20) SR_M01_0235_Sentosa [storyteller = Su; recipient = Yi]

((At the recording time of 02:35))

01	苏: Su:	我 说::, 那 你们: 今天 要 去玩 哪 wo shuo::, na nimen: jintian yao qu wan na I say then you today want go travel which
02		几个 景点 我 去哪 几- 那 几个: jige jingdian wo qu na ji- na jige: several scenery.spot I go which several that several
03		来 找 你 就 好了 嘛. .hh 然后 最后 她 lai zhao ni jiu haole ma. .hh ranhou zuihou ta come find you just ok PRT then finally she
04		就 说:, >什么< 圣淘沙 鱼尾狮 公园 jiu shuo:, >shenme< shengtaosha yuweishi gongyuan just say something Sentosa Merlion park
05		什么什么什 [么. .h shenmeshenmshen[me. .h so.on.and.so.forth *'I said::, then today which scenery spots would you visit, I could go to find you. .hh then finally she just said:, something like Sentosa the Merlion Park and so on.'*

06	易： Yi:	→	[话说 圣淘沙 是 什么 啊？ [huashuo shengtaosha shi shenme a? as.to Sentosa be what Q *'Talking about Sentosa what is it?'*
07	苏： Su:		圣淘沙 就是：(0.3) 在：[: shengtaosha jiushi: (0.3) zai:[: Sentosa that.is in *'Sentosa is: (0.3) in::'*
08	易： Yi:	→	[购物. [gouwu. shopping *'Shopping.'*
09	苏： Su:		不是，它 是 其实 [是 一个 海滩，= 你 知道 = bushi, ta shi qishi [shi yige haitan,= ni zhidao= no it be actually be one-CL beach you know *'No, actually it is a beach, you know='*
10	易： Yi:		[沙滩. [shatan sand.beach *'Sand beach.'*
11	苏： Su:		= 它 是 - .h 亚洲 :: 最南端. = ta shi- .h yazhou:: zuinanduan. it be Asia southernmost.point *'=It is the southernmost point of Asia.'*
12			((Su and Yi continue to discuss the geographic location of Sentosa and Singapore.

As can be seen in lines 1-2 Su asks the tour guide which scenery spots they would visit that day and expresses her intention to go to those spots to join her mother (lines 2 and 3). Su goes on to report that the tour guide told her that they would go 'places like Sentosa the Merlion Park and so on' (lines 3-5). When Su has not finished the utterance 'and so on' at line 5, Yi launches a question 'Talking about Sentosa what is it?' (line 6). This question shows that Yi may have heard of the name of Sentosa but has no idea what this place is[13]. Yi's question sidetracked Su's telling as her answer is made relevant in the next turn.

When Su starts to give an answer by saying 'Sentosa is: (0.3) in::' (line 7) her TCU-

⑬ Sentosa is a very popular playground tourist site in Singapore where there are a lot of attractions, beaches, and the theme park Universal Studio.

so-far projects a description of the place in terms of its geographic location. The sound stretch and pauses in her utterance shows her search of an appropriate word to name the location. Probably on seeing Su's problem in providing the answer, Yi supplies a single word 'Shopping' (line 8) showing her guess of what this place may be for. However, this tentative guess about Sentosa as a place for shopping is rejected by Su as she says 'No, actually it is a beach' (line 9).

Following Su's rejection of 'shopping' as the appropriate characterization of Sentosa, Yi supplies a second tentative item 'Sand beach' (line 10). This guess seems to be accepted by Su who herself also produces the same word 'sand beach' in her own utterance (line 9). The side sequence goes on for a while from this point onward, which is not included in the extract. However, from the expanded side sequence presented up to this far, it can already been seen that contingent on the way that the first turn in the side sequence is responded to, the side sequence may go beyond the minimal two or three turns.

Extract (4-21) below is another case where the side sequence is first expanded upon contingency emerging in the response made to the question that initiates the side sequence, and is further expanded by further contingencies as the side sequence progresses turn-by-turn.

(4-21) ES_M09_0115_Wednesday [storyteller = Cheng; recipient = Wei]

01	魏： Wei	哎 - 你 今天 早上 跟 我 说 那个： 就是 ai- ni jintian zaoshang gen wo shuo nage: jiushi hey you today morning with me say that-CL that.is
02		新西兰 的 那个 事儿 来 [着 xinxilan de nage shi'er lai [zhe New.Zealand PRT that-CL matther PRT *'Hey- you were saying the matter about New Zealand with me this morning.'*
03	程： Cheng	[对 啊 ::(.) [dui a::(.) right PRT *'Right'*
04		[就是 那天： 跟 :: (.).hh 跟： 啊 -(0.4) Tom(.) 就是 -k-= [jiushi natian: gen::(.).hh gen: a - (0.4) (.) jiushi-k-= that.is that.day with with Ah Tom that.is

05	魏 : Wei		[sh:- *[sh:-*
06	程 : Cheng		= 那天 就是 - 哎 :h (m- m-) 其实 也 不是 太 久 = natian jiushi- ai :h (m- m-) qishi ye bushi tai jiu that.day that.is INT actually also not too long
07			以 [前 哦 -. yi [qian o-. ago PRT *'Right it's on that day (I was) together with Ah Tom it's on that day, actually it's not a long time ago.'*
08	魏 : Wei	→	[星期 几 啊 .= [xingqi ji a.= days.of.the.week which Q *'What day (of the week) was that day.'*
09	程 : Cheng		= 我 后来 想起来 是 礼拜三 . = wo houlai xiangqilai shi libaisan.= I later remember be Wednesday *'Later I remembered that it was Wednesday.'*
10			(0.7)
11	魏 : Wei	→	礼拜三 ? (.) [上午 . libaisan? (.) [shangwu. Wednesday morning *'Wednesday?(.)Morning.'*
12	程 : Cheng		[应该 是 -(.) 应该 是 [礼拜三 , = 你 第一天 : [yinggai shi yinggai shi[libaisan, = ni diyitian should be should be Wednesday you first.day *'(It) should be- should be Wednesday,= the first day you'*
13	魏 : Wei	→	[啊 礼拜三 我 去 - [a libaisan wo qu- ah Wednesday I go
14			不 去 了 美领 [馆 了 嘛 . bu qu le meiling[guan le ma. not go ASP USA.Consulate ASP PRT *'Ah Wednesday I went- didn't I go to USA Consulate.'*
15	程 : Cheng		[对 : 你 一 天 天 - 第一天 [dui: ni yi tian tian- diyitian right you one day day first.day

16 去那 美领馆 的 [时候 .h > 我们 < 打 电话 =
qu na meilingguan de [shihou .h > women< da dianhua=
go that USA.Consulate PRT time we call telephone
'Right the first day when you went to USA Consulate, we called='

17 魏 : [对 啊 对 啊 .
Wei [dui a dui a.
right PRT right PRT
'Right right.'

18 程 : = 找 不到 你 嘛 ..hh[然后 :::(.) AA 说 要 吃饭 嘛 .
Cheng = zhao budao ni ma..hh[ranhou:::(.) shuo yao chifan ma
find not you PRT then AA say want have.dinner PRT
'=you but couldn't find you. And then AA asked to have dinner together.'

19 魏 : [° m hm°
Wei *[°m hm°*

20 (.)

21 魏 : ° m hm° =
Wei ° m hm° =

22 程 : = 然后 吃::: (0.3) 就:::: (0.5) 讲起 这件 事 了 嘛 ,
Cheng = ranhou chi::: (0.3) jiu:::: (0.5) jiangqi zhejian shi le ma,
then eat just mention this-CL thing ASP PRT
'And then we ate, and mentioned this thing,'

Extract (4-21) starts with Wei's inquiry to Cheng about 'that matter about New Zealand' she mentioned earlier that day (lines 1 and 2). Cheng begins by a vague reference to 'that day' when she discussed the matter with Tom. She does not seem to remember exactly on which day the matter was discussed but concludes it was not a long time ago (4, 6, and 7). When Cheng is just about to complete her utterance 'it's not a long time ago' (lines 6 and 7), Wei launches a question 'Which day (of the week) was that day' (line 8), apparently still interested in knowing the exact day when they discussed the matter. To this Cheng gives an answer 'Later I remembered that it was Wednesday' (line 9). After a noticeable 0.7-second gap (line 10), Wei responds with a repeat of 'Wednesday?' with a rising intonation, and when there is no immediate confirmation from Chen, she supplies another time reference 'morning' (line 11). Just as Wei is saying 'morning' Cheng simultaneously starts to respond to her 'Wednesday?'

with a confirmation. As soon as it is clear that Cheng's utterance-in-progress 'it should be …' (line 12) is giving a confirmation to 'Wednesday' (line 12), Wei quickly cuts in by saying 'Ah Wednesday I went- didn't I go to USA Consulate' (lines 13 and 14). This is Wei's own realization of what she did on Wednesday so that she missed their gathering.

Here, Wei's first question (line 8) about when the event happened occasions a side sequence within Cheng's telling as it obliges Cheng to produce a relevant answer in the next turn. When Cheng indeed does so, the course of her telling will have to be suspended, at least for the duration of the question-answer sequence. As it happens again, unlike the minimal sequence examined in Section 4.2, the first opportunity of going back to the suspended telling is not taken up by Cheng; nor does Wei produce a sequence-closing third. Instead, Cheng's provision of a time reference at line 9 ('Later I remembered it was Wednesday') prompts Wei to request confirmation on that time reference (line 11), which in effect moves the side sequence forward as the question-intoned repeat now makes relevant confirmation or disconfirmation in the next turn. Upon Cheng's confirmation, the opportunity to get back to the telling is again not taken up. Instead, Cheng's confirmation provides information for Wei to recall what she did on that Wednesday.

To summarize, this section explicates that emergent contingencies in the side sequence are interactional possibilities that are accountable for expanded and complex side sequences arising during the course of a telling sequence.

4.4.2 Side sequence expansion resulting from sequence design

In the current collection of side sequence within telling sequence, it is also found that some long side sequences are a result of sequence design where the story recipient's first side-sequence-initiating turn is produced with a sense of pre-ness as it projects further turns/action from the recipient. In general, the property of pre-ness can be characterized as something that "was done not as an action/move in its own right and analyzable in its own term alone, but for relevance to and bearing on some action/utterance projected to occur" (Schegloff, 2007, p. 28). When story recipient produces response with pre-ness, the ongoing telling is put at a higher risk of being derailed.

This section presents analysis of one extract where the side sequence is initiated by a turn with pre-ness, i.e. the responsive action in such a turn is preparatory to further talk by the recipient. As shown in (4-22) below, the story recipient's question which appears to be implementing a request for more details about the story-told-so-far turns out to be a 'pre' to a telling by the recipient herself.

Ren, the storyteller, has been telling that she had not been unwilling to be a teacher. But when she worked as a trainee teacher in a secondary school and was assigned to teach a class with poor students who had given up hope of taking the university entrance exams, she found herself becoming more committed and concerned, and started to encourage the students a lot. At the start of (4-22), Ren is telling that she would say lots of encouraging words to her students (lines 1 and 2).

(4-22) SR_M19_3206_Stage fright [storyteller = Ren; recipient Liu]

01 任 : 然后 会 跟 他们 说 很多 很多， .hh(.) 鼓励
Ren: ranhou hui gen tamen shuo henduo henduo,.hh(.) guli
then will with them talk many many encourage

02 他们 的 话 .
tamen de hua.
them PRT word
'And then I would talk to them with a lot of encouraging words.'

03 刘 : [((nodding, opens mouth))]
Liu:

04 任 : [((swallows))]
Ren:

05 任 : 然后 有 一天 晚上， .hhh (.) um::: (0.5) 我 就 ::
Ren: ranhou you yitian wanshang,.hhh (.) um::: (0.5) wo jiu::
then there.is one.day evening I then

06 说了 一节 课 吧 :, 就 大概 是 说 : <那个>,
shuo-le yi-jie ke ba:, jiu dagai shi shuo: <na-ge>,
talk-ASP one-CL class PRT just general be say that-CL

07 .hh 鼓励 的 一些 [话 .
.hh guli de yixie [hua.
encouraging PRT one-CL word
'And then one night, .hhh (.) um::: (0.5) I talked to them for a whole cla:ss, basically I was saying, .hh encouraging words.'

08 刘 : → [你 有没有 > 觉得 < 站到
Liu: [ni youmeiyou >juede< zhandao
you have-not-have feel stand-COMP

09			(.) 讲台 上面 觉得 你 怯场 . (.) jiangtai shangmian juede ni qiechang. platform on feel you stage.fright *'Did you >feel< when you stood (.) on the platform were you nervous.'*
10			(0.8)
11	任 : Ren:		不会 . buhui. no *'No.'*
12			(.)
13	刘 : Liu:		不会 .= buhui. no *'No.='*
14	任 : Ren:		= 我 会 很 享受 那种 感 [觉 . = wo hui hen xiangshou nazhong gan[jue. I will very enjoy that-CL feeling *'I enjoyed that feeling very much.'*
15	刘 : Liu:		[哇 : 这 说明 你 :: [wa: zhe shuoming ni :: INT this show you
16			你 的 (.) 那个 (.) 能力 还 是 很 强 . hhhhh ni de (.) nage (.) nengli hai shi hen qiang. hhhhh you PRT that-CL ability still is very strong
17		→	[因为 我 之前 就 做 老师 的 时候 ,= [yinwei wo zhiqian jiu zuo laoshi de shihou,= because I previously that.is be teacher PRT time *'Wa: this shows that you are very capable. hhhhh Because when I was a teacher,'*
18	任 : Ren:		[就 : < 很 喜欢 >. [jiu: <hen xihuan>. just very like *'Just like it very much.'*
19	刘 : Liu:		= 我 会 有点 怯场 , [因为 - = wo hui youdian qiechang, [yinwei- I will a.bit stage.fright because *'I have a little bit stage fright, because-'*

20 任：[啊，你 会 有点 紧张.
Ren: [a, ni hui youdian jinzhang.
INT you will a.bit nervous
'Ah, you are a bit nervous.'

21 刘： → 啊，对，因为 那么 ° 多° 学生 (.) 对着 我:,
Liu: a, dui, yinwei name ° duo° xuesheng(.) duizhe wo:,
INT right because that many student face-ASP me

22 而且 是 让 我 上 英语 课.=
erqie shi rang wo shang yingyu ke.=
and also be let me give English class
'Ah, right, because there were so many students sitting there, and I was asked to give an English class.'

23 ((Liu and Ren continue to talk about the aura of being a teacher.))

Then she goes into details about her saying encouraging words to the students in her class one evening (lines 5-7). At this point, Liu launches a question 'Did you have stage fright when you stood on the platform' (lines 8 and 9). Apparently, Liu's question inquires if Ren felt nervous when she spoke to her students on the platform, an issue not explicitly addressed in Ren's telling. Nevertheless, it is still relevant as an inquiry on an aspect in being a teacher. It could be a request for Ren to tell more about a particular aspect in teaching, i.e. having to speak to a whole class of students. But as their talk unfolds, it becomes clear that Liu's question is not a request in its own right.

Ren responds to Liu's question with *buhui* 'No' (line 11), and she further adds that she enjoyed standing on the platform very much (line 14). Following making an evaluation toward Ren's good feeling, Liu begins to share her own experience that when she was a teacher she had a little bit stage fright (lines 17 and 19). Liu further continues that the reason she had stage fright is that she was asked to give English class in front of many students (lines 21 and 22). Here, Liu's telling of her own experience explains why she launches the previous question about stage fright in lines 8 and 9. That is, Liu's previous question is not randomly targeting at one aspect of the told story. Because her question is designed in this way which is pre to her telling about the same issue, the occasioned side sequence gets further sidetracked.

4.4.3 Side sequence occasioned by storyteller's action

This section examines storyteller-initiated action within the side sequence that leads to the expansion of the side sequence. The data shows that on some occasions although the storyteller has an opportunity to close a side sequence or already closes it, he/she chooses to go back resulting in expanding the side sequence.

In the first example, (4-23), below, the storyteller tries to check whether what he has provided is sufficient enough to meet the story recipient's expectation. In the second example, (4-24), the storyteller initiatively provides more information about the issue in question.

Extract (4-23) is a continuation of Extract (4-21). Here Cheng is telling that it was while she was having lunch with other colleagues that they discussed possible places for students' study tour (lines 22-23).

(4-23) ES_M09_0138_ What did you eat [storyteller = Cheng; recipient = Wei]

22	程： Cheng		=然后 吃 ::: (0.3) 就 :::: (0.5) 讲起 这件 事 了 嘛， = ranhou chi ::: (0.3) jiu :::: (0.5) jiangqi zhejian shi le ma, then eat just mention this-CL thing ASP PRT
23			说 去 哪里 然后 就 - [我 就 提议 - shuo qu nali ranhou jiu- [wo jiu tiyi- talk go where then just I just suggest *'And then we ate, and mentioned this thing, talked about where to go and then I just suggested'*
24	魏： Wei	→	[哎 h 先 吃 什么 饭 先， [ai h xian chi shenme fan xian, INT first eat what meal first *'Ai what did you have for lunch first,'*
25			(.)
26	程： Cheng		.hh 去 -(.) 去 那个 叫 senior common room. .hh qu -(.) qu nage jiao go go that-CL call senior common room *'We went to that senior common room.'*
27			(0.3)

28 魏: > 好 啊 <(.) huh[吃 这个 好 啊 huh huh huh (xx) 我 huh huh huh
Wei > hao a <(.) huh[chi zhege hao a huh huh huh (xx) wo huh huh huh
great PRT eat this-CL great PRT I
'Great (.) huh it's great to eat there huh huh huh (xx) I huh huh huh'

29 程: [好 啊 huh huh huh huh huh huh huh huh huh 好 哇 .=
Cheng [hao a huh huh huh huh huh huh huh huh huh hao wa.=
great PRT great PRT
'Great huh huh huh huh huh huh huh huh huh great.'

30 魏: = 嗯 嗯 =
Wei *'=en en='*

31 程: =.hhh 然后: (0.4) ° AA 请吃饭° huh [huh huh huh huh huh
Cheng =.hhh ranhou: (0.4)° AA qingchifan° huh [huh huh huh huh huh
then AA's.treat
'And then: (0.4) it's AA's treat huh huh huh huh huh huh'

32 魏: [哦 - 好 啊 好 -huh huh 哦 h
Wei [o- hao a hao -huh huh o
oh great PRT great oh
'Oh- great great- huh huh oh'

33 (0.3)

34 程: → .hh 开始 - 吃 ::: 吃 什么 菜: 你 要 知道,
Cheng .hh kaishi- chi::: chi shenme cai: ni yao zhidao,
start eat eat what dish you want know
'We began- to eat::: do you want to know what we had for dinner,'

35 (.)

36 魏: 不是 我 就 想 知道 你们 去 哪里 ::::,=
Wei bushi wo jiu xiang zhidao nimen qu nali::::,=
no I just want know you go where
'No I just want to know where you ate,'

((Cheng and Wei continue to comment on the place Cheng had dinner.))

Just as Cheng is moving onto telling which place she suggested, Wei launches a question about what they had for dinner (line 24) triggering a side sequence where she inquires about what Cheng and other colleagues ate for lunch, although it is obvious from Cheng's telling up to this point that she is moving in the direction of recounting what they discussed over lunch rather than the kind of meal they had. At line 26 Cheng replies that they went to the senior common room (line 26). After a brief gap (line 27) during which Cheng does not show an attempt to get back to what suggestion she made at the lunch, Wei makes a positive assessment on the place they had dinner at (line 28, obviously displaying prior knowledge of the place) to which Cheng shows her affiliation (line 29). At this point, the side sequence is already expanded as both Wei and Cheng are engaged in giving assessment to the lunch place.

At line 31, Cheng produces the utterance ‘And then it’s AA’s treat’, again showing no sign to return to where her earlier telling was interrupted, i.e. where she was about to report what suggestion of the destination for students’ study tour she made at the discussion over lunch. Instead, she herself shows interest in staying on the topic of the lunch itself by telling Wei that the lunch was a treat from AA. After Wei responds with another positive assessment ‘Oh- great great- huh huh oh’ (line 32), there is a brief gap (line 33) after which Cheng starts with ‘we began to eat-’ which gives way to the question ‘do you want to know what we had for lunch’ (line 34). Examining Cheng’s utterance at line 34 in detail, it can be seen that when she starts to talk, lunch is still the topic of the talk. After her self-interruption, the question she asked further displays that she is very much into staying on the topic of lunch a little longer. Her question if Wei wants to know what dishes they had could be heard as showing an awareness that her earlier answer (i.e. they went to the common room) might be a potentially problematic one to Wei’s inquiry about what they ate for lunch, although Wei herself displays no trouble with it. Here, in terms of sequential organization, although Cheng has had opportunities to get back to telling what they did at lunch, she chooses to stay on the topic of the lunch itself and even initiates a question aiming at a potential problem in this topic. In this case, it is the teller of an earlier telling suspended by a side sequence who chooses to stay on the topic developed in the course of the side sequence. In other words, it is the teller’s contribution in the side sequence that expands it into an elaborate one. At this point whether the suspended telling will be resumed remains an open question.

Next, in (4-24), it is the storyteller who reopens the already closed side sequence and thus leads to a further sidetrack to the previous telling. This extract is taken from the same conversation of Extract 4-20. Recall in the analysis of (4-20) in Section 4.4.1, the storyteller Su’s recounting of her wish to join her mother’s tour group is interrupted by Yi’s question about what Sentosa is. Here, from line 1 to line 5, Yi and Su are talking about the geographic location of Sentosa. They are discussing whether Sentosa is the southernmost point of Asia.

(4-24) SR_M01_0346_Let me introduce more [storyteller = Su; recipient = Yi]

01 易 : 它的 意思 是不是 想 说 [< 亚欧板块 >,
Yi: tade yisi shibushi xiang shuo [<ya'oubankuai>,
its meaning be-not-be want say Asia-Europe.plate
'Does it mean the (southernmost point of) Aisa-Europe plate,'

02 苏 : [亚洲 大 :- 大陆
Su: [yazhou da:- dalu
Asian big continent

03 的 最南端 可能， [> 我 也 不 知道 < 哎 ::.=
de zuinanduan keneng, [>wo ye bu zhidao< ai::.=
PRT southernmost.point possible I also not know INT
'The southernmost point of Asian continent is possible, I have no idea either.'

04 易 : [这 还 差不多 .
Yi: [zhe hai chabuduo.
this still almost
'This is more like it.'

05 苏 : = 反正 他 [m-(.).h 那个 叫 西乐索 海滩 huh huh huh
Su: = fanzheng ta [m-(.).h nage jiao xilesuo haitan huh huh huh
anyway they that-CL call Siloso beach
'Anyway they- that's Siloso beach huh huh huh'

06 易 : [> 好 这 是 你的 故事 < (.) 圣淘沙 huh huh huh
Yi: [>hao zhe shi nide gushi < (.) shengtaosha huh huh huh
ok this be your story Sentosa
'Ok this is your story Sentosa huh huh huh'

07 Both: ((继续大笑))
((continue to laugh loudly))

08 苏 : → [.hhhh 好 - > 然后 她 -< 噢 - 那 我 现在 给 你 =
Su: [.hhhh hao- > ranhou ta- < ao- na wo xianzai gei ni=
ok then she ao- then I now for you

09 易 : [huh huh
Yi: *[huh huh*

10 苏 : = 介绍 一下 圣淘沙 好了 啊 , [然后 它 有 =
Su: = jieshao yixia shengtaosha haole a, [ranhou ta you=
introduce one-CL Sentosa good PRT then it have

11 易 : [mm
Yi: *[mm*

12 苏 : = 海滩 :, > 然 [后 < (.) hih::: 那 上面 还 - 修 了 个 =
Su: = haitan:, > ran[hou< (.) na shangmian hai- xiu le ge=
beach then that above also build ASP CL

13 易 : [mm hmh
Yi: *[mm hmh*

14 苏 : = universal studio.
Su: = universal studio.
'Ok- and then she- ao- now let me introduce Sentosa to you, and there is a beach, and there is universal studio.'

15 ((Su continues to proffer more information about Sentosa to Yi.))

At line 6, by saying 'ok this is your story (.) Sentosa', Yi proposes a closure to the rather expanded side sequence which is triggered by Yi's much earlier question about what Sentosa is. After Yi proposes the closure, both of them burst into laughter for a while (line 7). At line 8, Su first produces *hao* 'ok' which usually marks a disjunction between two topics, activities or actions (Miracle, 1989, 1991), seemingly accepting the proposed closure. Then Su appears to attempt to launch a recounting in saying 'ok- and then she-'. After she cuts off on *ta* 'she', Su does a repair and offers to introduce more about Sentosa 'let me introduce Sentosa to you' (lines 8 and 9).

Here, when Yi proposes a closure on the side sequence, Su first shows alignment to the proposal, but she quickly gives up on it through self-repair and decides to stay on the topic of Sentosa, and thus a side sequence on its possible closure is reopened.

4.5 Discussion and summary

To summarize, this chapter starts by sketching the sequential organization of recipient-initiated side sequences during storytelling. As examined in Section 4.2, such sequences are often organized in a two or three-turn structure (as illustrated in extracts 4-02 to 4-05, and schematized in tables 1-3). Two sequential positions are identified as the earliest possible points for getting back to halted telling. The first one is the second TCU in the second turn within the side sequence. The storyteller first produces a relevant response to recipient actions that triggers the side sequence, and stays on the turn by producing the next TCU in which the telling is resumed.

A: ongoing story

B: initiating side sequence

A: responding to B's action + returning to story

Or, the side sequence may run a three-turn sequence. In this sequence, it is the recipient who has initiated the side sequence proposes closing the sequence by producing a sequence-closing third (SCT) which does not contribute further topical talk in the side sequence. This provides the next earliest possible position for returning to his/her telling by the teller in the next turn following the recipient's SCT.

A: ongoing story

B: initiating side sequence

A: responding to B's action

B: producing SCT

A: returning to story

In Section 4.3, recipient responses which lead to side sequence is examined in terms of the actions they carry. The most frequent type of action is recipient's question which seeks details about an item not mentioned in the telling so far. Although recipient questions display their response to the telling, questions themselves are also first actions in terms of adjacency pair (Schegloff, 2007). So they also set up the relevance for an answer, and indeed all the questions asked by the story recipient are answered by the storyteller in the collected data.

A side sequence may also be occasioned by other types of action from the recipient, which can be seen as facilitating the telling, e.g. doing other repair and providing collaborative completion when storyteller exhibits problem in delivering the next bit of the story, or predicting the storyline. Although these actions are mainly supportive or facilitative in nature, they lead to side sequences as they make relevant the storyteller's confirmation or rejection in the next turn. Likewise, recipient actions such as displaying stance or showing understanding to the telling so far may also develop into side sequence if such actions are responded to by the storyteller.

In Section 4.4, the occurrence of expanded side sequence is examined. On certain occasions, a side sequence may get expanded due to contingencies arising during the course of it. On other occasions, an expanded side sequence is a result of sequence design when the side-sequence-initiating turn is produced as prelude to an upcoming action. Besides recipient expanded side sequences, the storyteller may also contribute to side sequence expansion when they choose to develop further talk within the side sequence.

In the next chapter, storytellers' practices in returning to halted telling will be examined.

Chapter 5

Returning to suspended story

5.1 Introduction

In the previous chapter, I showed that responsive actions from story recipients during an ongoing telling may lead to temporary suspension of that telling. In this chapter, I focus on how the storyteller returns to the suspended telling. Specifically, I describe the linguistic resources employed by storytellers. By analyzing frequently used techniques and the sequential position of their occurrence, I will show that storytellers make use of different techniques in returning to a story, including repetition, direct tying back, explicitly resuming search, etc..

Consider the following example (5-01), which will be analyzed in this section. In this extract, Ada is telling Bess about a friend of hers who first said she was full after a meal, but then wanted to eat again just a moment later. Here, the ongoing storytelling is halted when story recipient Bess makes an other-initiation in line 5, and the storyteller Ada returns to the halted story and resumes telling in lines 13 and 15 when the side sequence (lines 5 to 12) comes to completion.

(5-01) SR_M18_1638_Ham [storyteller = Ada; recipient = Bes]

01	ADA:	她 走到	那	下面	她 -	拿出	这 :: 么	粗
		ta zoudao	na	xiamian	ta-	nachu	zhe::me	cu
		she walk.to	that	downstairs	she	take.out	such	thick

02 一根 . (.) [她 说 , (0.8) 你 吃不吃 啊 ,=
yi-gen. (.) [ta shuo, (0.8) ni chi-bu-chi a, =
one-CL she say you eat-not-eat PRT
'She went downstairs and took out such a thick one.(.) She said, (0.8) do you want to eat it or not,'=

03 BES: [hmh
[hmh

04 ADA: =[我 说 ,
=[wo shuo,
I say
= '*I said,*'

05 BES: → [什么 东西 ?
[shenme dongxi?
what thing
'What is it?'

06 (.)

07 ADA: 火腿 啊 , (0.3) 那么 粗 一根 , [> 就是 - <
huotui a, (0.3) name cu yi-gen, [>jiushi- <
ham PRT such thick one-CL that.is
'Ham, (0.3) thick like this, >that is-<'

08 BES: [那 不 是 炒菜
[na bu shi chaocai
that not be cook

09 用 的 那种 .=
yong de na-zhong.=
use NOM that-kind
'Isn't that the kind used in cooking.='

10 ADA: => 哦 < 对 : (.) [就是 那 - huh huh
=> o < dui: (.) [jiushi na- huh huh
yeah right exactly that
='*>Yeah< ye:s (.) exactly that- huh huh*'

11 BES: [huh huh
[huh huh

12 (0.4)

13 ADA: → 她 > 实际上 < 就是 [想 : .hh 她 说 你
ta > shijishang< jiushi [xiang: .hh ta shuo ni
she actually just want she say you

14 BES: [huh
[huh

15 ADA: 吃不吃，= 我 说，(0.7) 不 吃． ((story continutes))
chi-bu-chi,= wo shuo, (0.7) bu chi.
eat-not-eat I say not eat
'She >actually< wanted: .hh she said, do you want to eat it or not, = I said, (0.7) no.' ((story continues))

Focusing on the phenomenon of 'returning', first, I investigate the devices employed by the storyteller for this purpose. As can be seen, Ada's returning in this case is accomplished by repetition of words said in the telling before its suspension due to the side sequence as evidenced in the repeated saying of 'she said do you want to eat it or not. I said,' (lines 2, 4 and 13, 15). Repetition is one of the linguistic devices through which storyteller gets back to suspended telling. In Section 5.2 this will be examined together with three other devices for returning to prior telling after the close of side sequence. Second, I examine the interactional motivations for successful returnings. Some stories may be told more or less just for the sake of sharing without extra loaded interactional purposes. Returning to suspended stories like this displays the teller's insistence on bringing the story to completion, i.e. to present the recipient with a complete recount of a past experience or event. Other stories may be told for certain interactional purposes. As mentioned earlier in Section 2.2.2, stories told in conversation may serve as vehicles for other actions in interaction, e.g. complaining, boasting, informing, alerting, teasing, explaining, justifying, etc. (Schegloff, 1997). In such cases returning to a suspended story is a means of completing the action carried by that story.

As shown in the previous chapter, the side sequence can either be a minimal one that permits an easy return to the prior telling, or an expanded one that runs into several turns (or more) resulting from either sequence design of the recipients' response or contingencies arising in the side sequence. This chapter mainly focuses on returnings subsequent to an expanded side sequence.

The chapter is organized in two main parts: Section 5.2 presents analysis of the strategies found in the teller's practice of returning to suspended story. Section 5.3 discusses the interactional functions of returning. Section 5.4 presents an interim summary of the chapter.

5.2 Practices used in doing returning

My analysis of the cases in the current data set reveals that: (1) returnings can be implemented by repeating certain part in the story that immediately preceded the halting of the telling; (2) returnings can be achieved by directly tying back to the previously halted storytelling by producing the next bit as projected by the telling up to its suspension; (3) the storyteller may pre-indicate an imminent return when he/she is still in the side sequence; and (4) on certain occasions, extra effort needs to be made to pursue a returning, such as doing a resuming search, insisting on continuing the story, etc.. In this section, the practices used by the storyteller in managing storytelling returns are analyzed.

5.2.1 Repetition

In conversation, some utterances are heard or analyzed as ‘repeats’ of previous utterances (Schegloff, 1997). Schegloff (1996) not only discriminates between repeats produced by the same speaker and those produced by the second speaker, but also points out that repetition can occur in the turn immediately following the utterance to be repeated, or in any subsequent turn. As summarized by Wong (2000)[14], various actions are accomplished when one repeats another person’s utterance: this action may initiate repair, register receipt, signal rejection, correction, or disalignment (Pomerantz, 1984), or confirm allusions (Schegloff, 1996).

As pointed out by Ochs, Schegloff, and Thompson (1996), recycled utterances at different linguistic levels (including words, phrases, clauses and sentences) can “create conjunctive or cohesive relations as well and perhaps do some more effectively and efficiently than do their traditional counterparts in a convergence of everyday language, grammar, turn taking, and repair” (cited in Wong, 2000, p. 416).

The current data shows that repetition can also be used by the storyteller to

⑭ Wong (2000) investigates same turn repetition by the same speaker and shows that this repetition can be used as a practice to do storytelling resumption after self-interruption. Her study is different from mine in the sense that the storytelling in her study is self-interrupted and the repetition occur within the same turn of the first saying, while in the cases I focus on, the ongoing storytelling becomes halted because of the story recipient’s action and the repeat occurs in the subsequent turn by another speaker, i.e. the storyteller.

accomplish a storytelling resumption. By repeating particular components or units of the story suspended due to side sequence, the storyteller can tie back to and ultimately return to the halted storytelling.

Extract (5-01) briefly examined above is a case in point. It is reproduced below as (5-02). Recall the suspension of the telling is triggered by a repair sequence working on a vague reference term. The returning in this case is accomplished through repetition.

(5-02) SR_M18_1638_Ham [storyteller = Ada; recipient = Bes]

01 ADA: 她 走到 那 下面 她 - 拿出 这 :: 么 粗
ta zoudao na xiamian ta- nachu zhe::me cu
she walk.to that downstairs she take.out such thick

02 一根 . (.) [她 说 , (0.8) 你 吃不吃 啊 ,=
yi-gen. (.) [ta shuo, (0.8) ni chi-bu-chi a,=
one-CL she say you eat-not-eat PRT
'She went downstairs and took out such a thick one.(.) She said, (0.8) do you want to eat it or not,'=

03 BES: [hmh
[hmh

04 ADA: =[我 说 ,
=[wo shuo,
I say
='I said,'

05 BES: → [什么 东西 ?
[shenme dongxi?
what thing
'What is it?'

06 (.)

07 ADA: 火腿 啊 , (0.3) 那么 粗 一 根 , [> 就是 - <
huotui a, (0.3) name cu yi-gen, [>jiushi- <
ham PRT such thick one-CL that.is
'Ham, (0.3) thick like this, >that is-<'

08 BES: [那 不 是 炒菜
[na bu shi chaocai
that not be cook

09 用 的 那 种 .=
yong de na-zhong.=
use NOM that-kind
'Isn't that the kind used in cooking.='

10 ADA: => 哦< 对: (.) [就是 那 - huh huh
=> o < dui: (.) [jiushi na - huh huh
yeah right exactly that
= '>Yeah< ye:s (.) exactly that- huh huh'

11 BES: [huh huh
[huh huh

12 (0.4)

13 ADA: → 她 >实际上< 就是 [想: .hh 她 说 你
ta >shijishang< jiushi [xiang: .hh ta shuo ni
she actually just want she say you

14 BES: [huh
[huh

15 ADA: 吃不吃,= 我 说, (0.7) 不 吃. ((story continutes))
chi-bu-chi,= wo shuo, (0.7) bu chi.
eat-not-eat I say not eat
'She >actually< wanted: .hh she said, do you want to eat it or not, = I said, (0.7) no.' ((story continues))

As shown in the earlier analysis, the side sequence results from Bess' request to work on a reference problem in Ada's telling as evidenced by her other-initiaiton (line 5) on a vague expression 'a thick one'. Close examination shows that the side sequence develops into an expanded one when Bess asks another question (line 8). After the storyteller Ada gives a positive response to Bess' follow up question in line 10, Ada repeats 'She >actually wanted: .hh she said, do you want to eat it, = I said, (0.7) no.' (lines 13 and 15), showing that she is returning to her telling, that is, back to where she was recounting the conversation between her friend and her and then continues from there. The resumption is achieved through almost-verbatim repetition of the reported conversation between her friend and her 'she said, (0.8) do you want it,=I said' (lines 2 and 4). As repetition of some part in prior telling connects the current turn with the prior by sharing a similar part, it is an explicit way of returning to the suspended telling.

In the next example, the storyteller also repeats a bit of what was said before the interruption. Interestingly, when the side sequence comes to a possible completion point, the teller does a repair and then uses her turn to repeat what she said before.

The next extract (5-03), is a similar example where returning to prior telling after an expanded side sequence is accomplished through repetition of words said before the telling was suspended. The storyteller in the extract, Lena has been recounting her stay in a friend's dorm during her trip in Beijing. She has told Tina that it was very hot because the window could only be opened halfway and the mattress was too thick. The extract begins with Lena saying that her classmates and her mother slept very well (lines 1-2).

(5-03) ES_M11_0918_No power supply [storyteller = Lena; recipient = Tina]

01 LEN: 然后：-(0.4) 她 - 我 不 知道 我 同学 她们 都 睡
ranhou:-(0.4) ta - wo bu zhidao wo tongxue tamen dou shui
then she I not know my classmate they all sleep

02 得 很 好 .(0.3).h 我 [妈 :: 她 也 睡 得 很 好 .
de hen hao.(0.3).h wo [ma:: ta ye shui de hen hao.
PRT very good my mother she also sleep PRT very good
'And the:n- (0.4) she- I don't know how come my classmates slept so well. (0.3). h My mother also slept very well.'

03 TIN: [你 还 : 觉得 很 热 .
[ni hai: juede hen re
you still feel very hot
'You sti:ll felt very hot.'

04 LEN: .hh 而且 他们 晚上 是 没 有 电 的 嘛 .=
.hh erqie tamen wanshang shi mei you dian de ma.=
and.also they night be not have electricity PRT PRT
'.hh And they didn't have power supply at night.='

05 TIN: → =(° xx°) 哦 :[: ? 这样 的 啊 .
=(° xx°) o :[:? zheyang de a.
oh this-CL PRT Q
'=(°xx°)Oh::? Like this ah.'

06 LEN: [就 限 电 的 > 嘛 <. = 对 , 大学
[jiu xian dian de >ma <. = dui, daxue
just restrict electricity PRT PRT right university

07 本科 都 是 限 电 的 .(.).h[> 然后 -<
benke dou shi xian dian de.(.).h [> ranhou-<
undergraduate all be restrict electricity PRT then
'Just restricted power supply.=Yeah, there was restriction on power supply in undergraduate students' dorm.(.).h >And then-<'

08 TIN: [我们
[women
we

09 不是 啊 hmh hmh hmh
bushi a hmh hmh hmh
not PRT
'We were not like that hmh hmh hmh'

10 LEN: 哦 - 我 - 我 - 你们 : 你们 已经 是 后面 几年
o - wo- wo- nimen: nimen yijing shi houmian jinian
oh I I you you already be afterwards several-year

11 了 ,= 已经 很 [好 了,= 我们 那 时候 都 是 =
le ,= yijing hen [hao le,= women na shihou dou shi =
PRT already very good PRT we that time all be

12 TIN: [> 噢 噢 噢 噢 <
[>ao ao ao ao<
'>Ao ao ao ao<'

13 LEN: = 十二 点 以后 就 关灯 的 .
= shi'er dian yihou jiu guandeng de.
twelve o'clock after just turn.off.light PRT
'Oh- I- I- you: you were in a few years later,=it's already very good,=our light was turned off at twelve o'clock.'

14 (0.3)

15 LEN: → .hh 就是 限- (.) 就 没 有 电 了 . =
.hh jiushi xian- (.) jiu mei you dian le. =
that.is restrict that.is no have electricity PRT
'.hh That's the restrict- (.) that's no power supply.='

16 TIN: =.hhh[(好) 惨 (呐).
=.hhh[(hao) can (na).
very tragic PRT
'=.hhh So tragic.'

17 LEN: [然后 - 我 一个 人 很 热 .(0.3) 然后 我 就
[ranhou- wo yige ren hen re. (0.3) ranhou wo jiu
then I one-CL person very hot then I just

18 去 把 他们 那 - 外面 那个 (.) 外面 那 块
qu ba tamen na- waimian nage (.) waimian na-kuai
go BA their that outside that-CL outside that-piece

19 走廊 的 一块 地方 s- (0.7) 扫扫 干 (h) 净 (h),
zoulang de yi-kuai difang s- (0.7) saosao gan(h) jing(h),
corridor PRT one-piece place sweep clean
'And then- I myself felt very hot. (0.3) And then I just went out of the dorm and s-swept a place in the corridor,' ((story continues))

Tina then makes a prediction of the storyline 'You sti:ll felt very hot' (line 3), showing her guess of where the course of Lena's telling might be going (lines 1-2). However, this prediction receives no uptake from Lena as she continues with a report of the circumstance in which they slept: 'And they didn't have power supply at night' (line 4) to which Tina responds with 'oh::? Like this ah.' (line 5) showing a bit of disbelief about the lack of power supply in a hot summer night. This leads to a side sequence where Lena explains that by no power supply she meant restricted power supply, and she also adds that power supply in all undergraduates' dorms was restricted (lines 6-7). The side sequence is further expanded when Tina offers a contrast: 'We were not like that' (lines 8-9) apparently taking issue with the inclusive quantifier 'all' in Lena's explanation of restricted power supply. Responding to this implicit disagreement, Lena points out the different time periods of their university years, i.e. Tina went to university in more recent years when power supply must have been improved, but during Lena's undergraduate years the light was turned off every night at twelve (lines 10, 11, and 13).

After a 0.3-second pause, Lena produces the utterance 'that's the restrict- (.) that's no power supply' (line 15), which appears at first to be a further explanation of the turning off of the light. Lena's subsequent 'And then- I myself felt very hot. (0.3) And then I just went out of the dorm and s- swept a place in the corridor,' (lines 17-19) shows she is returning to her prior telling (lines 1, 2, and 4).

Focusing on Lena's utterance at line 15, we can see that she begins with 'that's the restrict-', possibly intended as a summary or generalization of her (line 7) explanation of restricted power supply applied to undergraduates' dorms. But she self-interrupts and re-starts with 'that's no power supply', clearly repeating her utterance earlier at line 4. Critical for our purposes here is that, in performing this repair, Lena makes an effort to change her words from *jiushi xian-* 'restriction of (power)' to *meiyou dian* 'no power', thus directly repeating her utterance from line 4 in order to resume the halted telling.

In the example below, when coming out of the side sequence the storyteller also repeats a bit of what was said earlier as a means to continue telling by picking up from where the telling was suspended. Prior to extract (5-04), Rui is telling Li the requirements of a course she took which includes making notes, writing a final paper, participating in discussion, etc..

(5-04) ES_M04_0715_Having dinner [storyteller = Rui; recipient = Li]

01 芮 : 然后 闲扯 :, .h 然后 会 - 会 讲
Rui ranhou xianche:, .h ranhou hui- hui jiang
then chat then will will talk

02 很 长 时间 , .h 然后 (xxx-) 然后 就 - (0.3)
hen chang shijian,.h ranhou (xxx-) ranhou jiu- (0.3)
very long time then then just

03 但 - 只要 你 参加 过 那 以后 基本上 就是
dan- zhiyao ni canjia guo na yihou jibenshang jiushi
but only you join ASP that after basically that.is

04 那 课堂 讨论 分 他 会 - 都 会 给 你 了 ,
na ketang taolun fen ta hui- dou hui gei ni le,
that class discussion mark he will all will give you ASP

05 .h 然 [后 - n:
.h ran [hou- n:
then
'And then all the people began to talk and chat freely for a long time, .h and then (xxx-) and then just- (0.3) but- as long as you joined that dinner basically he would give you marks for class discussion, .h and then- n:'

06 李 : → [参加 过 吃饭 就 给 [° 分° . (.) [huh huh
Li [canjia guo chifan jiu gei [° fen° . (.) [huh huh
join ASP have.dinner just give marks
'Gave you marks after having dinner. huh huh'

07 芮 : [对 对 (x-) [因为
Rui [dui dui (X-) [yinwei
right right because

08 你 要 先 在 论坛 上 (.) 灌很多水
ni yao xian zai luntan shang (.) guanhenduoshui
you need first in forum in send.many.posts

09 他 才 会 请 你 [去 . huh
ta cai hui qing ni [qu. huh
he only will invite you go
'Right right (x-) because you need to send many posts in the forum he would only invite you after that. huh'

10 李 : [哦 :::::?=
Li [o:::::?=
oh
'Oh::::::?='

11 芮 : → =.h 然后 最后 那篇 论文 也 很 搞笑 然后 -,
Rui =.h ranhou zuihou napian lunwen ye hen gaoxiao ranhou-,
then last that-CL paper also very funny then

12 因为 那 课, = 选 那 课 的 人 有
yinwei na ke, = xuan na ke de ren you
because that course choose that course NOM people have

13 好多 理科 背景 的 人, ((story continues))
haoduo like beijing de ren,
a.lot.of science background NOM people
'=And then the last paper was also very funny and then-, because that course was taken by many students who had background in science,' ((story continues))

As analyzed in Section 4.3.4 when much of the extract was presented as (4-15), Rui's recount of the requirement of a course she took was interrupted by a side sequence initiated by Li. Through reformulation, she shows her understanding of the telling about receiving marks for class participation after having dinner with the teaching assistant. The analytical focus here is how Rui gets back to her telling when the side sequence comes to completion. For this, let us look at lines 5 and 11 again to examine the last word said before the suspension of the telling and the first word when the story is resumed.

Let us first examine line 5. Here Rui's last word in the telling-so-far is *ranhou* 'and then'. Let us further examine line 5 in relation to lines 3-4 and line 6. It can be seen that the TCU (begun in line 3) with which Rui reports how one would receive marks for class participation has come to possible completion at the end of line 4 ('*but- as long as you joined that dinner basically he would give you marks for class discussion'*). Then in line 5 Rui continues onto the next TCU with the connective *ranhou* 'and then', clearly indicating moving onto the next bit in the telling. As it turns out, Li comes in on the second syllable of Rui's connective when she starts her reformulation in line 6. This overlap is brief as Rui gives up continuing from the connective.

Now let us examine line 11. The first word said by Rui is the same connective *ranhou* 'and then'. Prior to this, Rui's utterance at lines 7-9 is her response to Li's reformulation. It comes to possible completion at the end of line 9. At this point if Rui continues to talk, there may be alternative routes. She could choose to stay on her explanation by producing further talk along this line, or she could choose to move out of the side sequence. Here, the connective at the beginning of line 11 is ambiguous in this regard as it indicates continuation without specifying in which direction the new TCU is going. However, as she was interrupted on the connective, when she repeats it at a possible completion point in the side sequence, the possibility of using repetition for getting back to prior telling is high. As can be seen from what follows the connective at line 11 (*'And then the last paper was also very funny*) it is clear that Rui is picking up from where she was interrupted back at line 5, and is continuing onto the next requirement for the course, i.e. the final paper, which she characterizes as funny. Here Rui's resumption to prior telling is facilitated by a repetition of the connective which locates where her telling got interrupted earlier. The repeating of *ranhou* 'and then' here is similar to what is reported by Koenig (2005): the repetition of the last component that occurred before the oblique sequence shows a resumption of the on-hold project[⑮]. In another words, although the component being repeated is very brief and contains no narrated event, it can nevertheless indicate a storytelling resumption.

The above three examples (5-02, 5-03, and 5-04) show that returning to halted storytelling can be achieved through repetition of particular components of the interrupted story. The returning in extract (5-02) is achieved through the repetition of a reported conversation; in extract (5-03), the returning is achieved by manipulating the closure of the side sequence to repeat one component in the interrupted story; in extract (5-04), the returning is initiated through the repetition of the connective *ranhou* 'and then' which locates the point of interruption.

Although what is repeated by the storyteller varies, the repetitions are closely related to the sequential and interactional environment in which the ongoing storytelling was halted. For instance, comparing extracts (5-02) and (5-04), prior to the occurrence of the side sequence, the storyteller in extract (5-04) has finished describing one requirement of the course, and the use of *ranhou* 'and then' possibly projects her intention to begin describing another requirement of that course; in extract (5-02), the storyteller is interrupted while she is recounting the conversation between story

⑮ In Koenig's (2009) study, he investigates the multi-unit-turn environment, not just storytelling sequences. His focus in that study is the organization of question-initiated oblique sequences. He also addresses how people return to the on-hold project when the oblique sequence comes to its completion point.

characters 'She said, (0.8) do you want to eat it,=I said' (lines 2 and 4, extract 5-02). The sequential and interactional environment in which the storytelling became halted can thus offer an explanation as to why the storyteller in extract (5-04) only repeats the connective ranhou 'and then', while the storyteller in extract (5-02) repeats a larger portion in prior telling to achieve resumption. In the case of (5-04), it is unlikely that the storyteller would repeat part of the already finished component (which occurred prior to *ranhou* 'and then'), whereas in (5-02), the telling is interrupted when the reporting of the conversation is still in progress. In this case repeating the partially reported conversation helps to preserve the completeness of the recounting of that conversation between story characters as well as indicating resumption to prior telling to the story recipient. The storyteller's repetition in extract (5-03) also shows a repetition that is relevant to the local sequential and interactional environment: the storyteller makes use of the turn she holds and designs the closure of the side sequence as a repetition of one component in the interrupted story.

As shown in the above discussion, storytelling resumption achieved through the repetition of particular components of the story-on-hold is not randomly accomplished. Rather, the storyteller's repetition is an ordered and systematic practice that is closely relevant to the sequential and interactional environment.

5.2.2 Direct continuation

The storyteller may also return to the halted telling by directly continuing from where he/she stopped. That is, upon completion of the side sequence, the storyteller can produce the next possible story element and return directly to prior telling. In doing direct continuation, *ranhou* ('and then') is a pervasive initiator[16].

According to grammar of Chinese sentences, *ranhou* ('and then'), is a "temporal conjunction", used to indicate that one event occurs after the previous event (Lü, 1980, p. 461). That is, the use of *ranhou* ('and then') underlines the actual temporal progression among events. However, *ranhou* ('and then') has gradually developed non-temporal functions (Fang, 2000; Xu, 2009; Biq, 2010): it may signal the holding of an extended turn (Fang, 2000), mark a list of items and open a topic (Xu, 2009), and organize

⑯ Note that, while I suggest that *ranhou* ('and then') is a particularly pervasive initiator, I am not arguing that all continuations must begin with this item.

sequential progression of the discourse (Biq, 2010), etc.. *Ranhou* ('and then') also frequently occurs in storytelling sequences, where it is used as a connective to organize the actual temporal progression of the events being narrated as well as to manage the linear arrangement of the components in the telling.

Direct continuation is one of the most frequently used methods by which a storyteller returns to halted telling, especially after a minimal side sequence as in the example below (5-05). Prior to this extract, Lena, the storyteller, has been telling Tina that she visited many places in Beijing on a trip there with her family and is now describing their visit to the Thirteen Tombs of the Ming Dynasty.

(5-05) ES_M11_0513_Thirteen Tombs [storyteller = Lena; recipient = Tina]

01 LEN: 我们 当时 是 下午 四十 度 唉:, (.)
women dangshi shi xiawu sishi du ai:, (.)
we at.that.time be afternoon forty degree PRT

02 .h 我们 先 是 去 参观 那个:: (0.8) 十三: 水-
.h women xian shi qu canguan na-ge:: (0.8) shisan: shui-
we first be go visit that-CL thirteen water
'When we were there it was forty degrees in the afternoon,(.).h we first went to visit tha::t (0.8) Thirtee:n water-'

03 (.)

04 TIN: → 十三陵.=
shisanling.=
Thirteen.Tombs
'Thirteen Tombs.='

05 LEN: =哎-, 十三陵.=
= ai-, shisanling.=
INTJ Thirteen.Tombs
='Yeah-, Thirteen Tombs.'=

06 TIN: =噢.
=ao.
INTJ
'=Ao.'

07 (0.3)

08 LEN: → >然后< 十三 陵 >好像< 去 了 两个 吧, [.hh=
> ranhou< shisan ling > haoxiang< qu le liangge ba, [.hh=
then thirteen tomb likely go ASP two-CL PRT
'>And then< we went to about two of the Thirteen Tombs,.hh='

09 TIN: [mm
'[mm'

10 LEN: =上午 去十三 陵 然后 再: .h(.) = 我们
= shangwu qu shisan ling ranhou zai: .h(.) = women
morning go thirteen tomb then then we

11 当时 参加 了 一日游 (h) 了 (h).
dangshi canjia le yiriyou (h) le (h).
at.that.time join ASP one.day.tour ASP
'=In the morning we went to the Thirteen Tombs and the:n .h (.) = at that time we joined a one-day tour.'

As discussed in chapter 4, a side sequence within Lena's story is occasioned by the story recipient's initiation of an other-repair, 'Thirteen Tombs' (line 4), which targets the storyteller's trouble source 'Thirtee:n water-' (line 2). When the repair sequence is complete with Tina's acknowledgement (line 6), Lena utters '>And then< we went to about two of the Thirteen Tombs,' (line 8) indicating that she is returning to the telling about their visit to the Thirteen Tombs.

If we look at the connection between the halting of the story and the resumption, we can see that the second shaded part (line 8) in extract (5-05) appears to be a continuation of the first shaded part (line 2). That is, when the side sequence comes to its possible completion, the storyteller directly ties back to her previously halted storytelling by launching into the next component of her story - the details of their traveling in the Thirteen Tombs (line 8). Here, *ranhou* is employed as a discourse marker (rather than a temporal connective). If we omit the side sequence, the story develops as follows:

(5-05b)

02 LEN: .h 我们 先 是 去 参观 那个 :: (0.8) 十三 : 水 -
.h women xian shi qu canguan na-ge:: (0.8) shisan: shui-
we first be go visit that-CL thirteen water
.h We first went to visit tha::t (0.8) Thirtee:n water-'

⋯ ⋯ ((omitted side sequence, 5 lines))

08 LEN: >然后< 十三 陵 >好像< 去 了 两个 吧 ,[.hh=
> ranhou< shisan ling >haoxiang< qu le liangge ba, [.hh=
then thirteen tomb likely go ASP two-CL PRT
'>And then< we went to about two of the Thirteen Tombs,.hh='

Thus, Lena continues the storytelling as if it proceeds without the intervening side sequence.

Direct continuation is a frequently used method of resuming a halted telling not only after a minimal side sequence, but also after an expanded side sequence. The following example (extract 5-06) shows how a teller returns to prior telling through continuation after a rather expanded side sequence.

The following example is extracted from a three-party conversation. As I analyzed in the previous chapter, the storyteller Lin's storytelling (lines 1-4) about an experience of eating mangosteen gets halted when one of the story recipients, Fen, expresses a different opinion (line 5) from the reported opinion of one story character (Lin's mother). Lin later returns to the halted telling by directly continuing the story with the next story element (lines 18-19).

(5-06) SR_M09_0605_Mangosteen [storyteller = Lin; recipient = Fen and Wan]

01	琳: Lin:		那个 时候, (.) 我们 去马来西亚 的 时候, (.) 我 妈 nage shihou,(.) women qu malaixiya de shihou,(.) wo ma that-CL time we go Malaysia PRT time my mother
02			就-她-我 就 很 喜欢 吃 我 就 说 啊:: jiu- ta- wo jiu hen xihuan chi wo jiu shuo a:: just she I just very like eat I then say INT
03			我们 吃 这个 吧, (.) 然后 我 妈 就-看 这个 women chi zhege ba, (.) ranhou wo ma jiu- kan zhege we eat this-CL PRT then my mother just look this-CL
04			样子 就 觉得 不 好吃 嘛.= yangzi jiu juede bu haochi ma.= look just think not delicious PRT *'When my mother and I went to Malaysia,(.)my mother- just-she- I really like it and I said, 'Ah:: let's have it',(.)and then my mother thought it would not be delicious because of its look.='*
05	芬: Fen:	→a	=超 好吃 的.= =chao haochi de.= super delicious PRT *'=It's super delicious.='*
06	琳: Lin:		=对 啊 我 觉得 [好 好吃 的. = dui a wo juede [hao haochi de. right PRT I think very delicious PRT *'Right, I think it's very delicious.'*

07 芬: [前- 我 觉得 很 像 大蒜 huh[huhhuh
Fen: [qian- wo juede hen xiang dasuan huh[huhhuh
before I think very like garlic huhhuhhuh
'I used to think it looks like garlic huh huh huh'

08 琳: [<对 啊>.
Lin: [<dui a>.
right PRT

09 哎(.)吃 咯, 吃 咯. (1.2)你 是 不 喜欢 吃 吗?
ai (.) chi lo, chi lo. (1.2) ni shi bu xihuan chi ma?
INT eat PRT eat PRT you be not like eat Q
'Right. Ai, have some, have some.(1.2)Don't you like it?'

((6 lines are omitted, during which, Fen answers that Wan also likes it. Wan herself said it is because she hasn't finished her leechee. Lin continues to offer the fruit.))

16 琳: =哦:.(0.8)还有 吃 这些.((gives Fen a peeled mangosteen))
Lin: = o :.(0.8) haiyou chi zhexie.
oh also eat these
'Oh:.(0.8) Have these as well.'((gives Fen a peeled mangosteen))

17 (3.1) ((Lin throws the shuck into trash can))

18 琳: →b 然后 (.)后来 最后 我 就 吃 完 之后 就
Lin: ranhou(.) houlai zuihou wo jiu chi wan zhihou jiu
then later finally I just eat finish after just

19 好像 有一点, (0.4)不知道 怎么: 有点 那个, (.)
haoxiang youyidian,(0.4) buzhidao zenme: youdian nage, (.)
seem a.bit not.sure how a.bit that-CL

20 然后 我 妈 就 说 (.)是不是 那个.
ranhou wo ma jiu shuo (.) shibushi nage.
then my mother just say be.not.be that-CL
'And then (.) later finally after finishing eating it, it just seemed I was a little bit, (0.4) I'm not sure how come I was a little bit that, (.) and then my mother said (.) 'whether it is that'.'

The detailed analysis of the extract in chapter 4 shows that Lin's story is interrupted when Fen's remark 'It's super delicious' (line 5) leads to a side sequence in which the focal activity is on the taste of mangosteen. Unlike the minimal side sequence in (5-05), the side sequence here becomes more expanded because of the story recipient's follow-up comment on the shape of mangosteen, 'I used to think it looks like garlic' (line 7), and gets further expanded because Lin invites them all to have more mangosteen (line 9).

The side sequence finally reaches its completion after Lin offers more mangosteen to the story recipient in line 16 and then says, 'And then (.) later finally after finishing eating it, it just seemed I was a little bit, (0.4) I'm not sure how come I was a little bit like that' (lines 18-19). This transition shows that Lin is returning to her prior storytelling about eating mangosteen. Lin's utterance 'after finishing eating mangosteen' (line 18) is a direct continuation of her earlier recounting (lines 2, 3 and 4) before the side sequence (beginning at line 5). Here, Lin returns to the previously halted story as if the next component in the storyline goes directly from where she was interrupted:

(5-06b)

02	琳：		我 就 很 喜欢 吃 我 就 说 啊 ::
	Lin:		wo jiu hen xihuan chi wo jiu shuo a::
			I just very like eat I then say INT
03			我们 吃 这个 吧 ,(.) 然后 我 妈 就 - 看 这个
			women chi zhege ba,(.) ranhou wo ma jiu- kan zhege
			we eat this-CL PRT then my mother just look this-CL
04			样子 就 觉得 不 好吃 嘛 .=
			yangzi jiu juede bu haochi ma.=
			look just think not delicious PRT
			I really like it and then said, 'Ah:: let's have it',(.)and then my mother thought it would not be delicious because of its look.='
			…… ((omitted side sequence, 13 lines))
18	琳：	→	然后 (.) 后来 最后 我 就 吃 完 之后 就
	Lin:		ranhou(.) houlai zuihou wo jiu chi wan zhihou jiu
			then later finally I just eat finish after just
19			好像 有一点， (0.4) 不知道 怎么 : 有点 那个， (.)
			haoxiang youyidian,(0.4) buzhidao zenme: youdian nage, (.)
			seem a.bit not.sure how a.bit that-CL
			'And then (.) later finally after finishing eating it, it just seemed I was a little bit, (0.4) I'm not sure how come I was a little bit that,(.)

Here, the returning is again accomplished through direct continuation. Unlike the previous example (extract 5-05) where the continuation offers further details of their visit to the Thirteen Tombs, the continuation in this example (5-06) follows the temporal sequence of the events recounted in the story. That is, what is recounted by the storyteller before the interruption — her own proposal to her mother to have mangosteen together (lines 2-3) and her mother's suspicious feeling of the fruit (lines 3-4) — happened in this temporal sequence before they actually ate the fruit; the continuation of the story after the interruption picks up the temporal sequence of the events i.e. the telling reports what happened after they ate the mangosteen (lines 18-19)[17].

Similar to the above two examples, the next example (5-07) also shows how returning is achieved through direct continuation. Although the storyteller's telling is later blocked because of the story recipient's follow-up action, the returning attempt through continuation is still clear.

Prior to this extract, the storyteller Lena has been telling Tina that they asked one of their friends in Beijing to take photos in different locations according to the four seasons of the year and send the photos to them. That is, a list of sightseeing spots is projected in the beginning of the story.

(5-07) ES_M11_0831_Photo [storyteller = Lena; recipient = Tina]

01 LEN: .h 他 有 一次 给 我们 寄来 那个 (.) 北 (.) 大
.h ta you yici gei women ji-lai nage (.) bei (.) da
he have one.time to us mail-COMP that-CL Peking.U

02 的 那个 z-(.) < 秋天 的 草坪 >, .hh 就 看到
de nage z-(.) <qiutian de caoping>, .hh jiu kan-dao
PRT that-CL autumn PRT lawn just see-COMP

03 黄压 [压 的 .
huangya[ya de.
yellow.mass PRT
'.h Once he sent us the photo of <the lawn in Autumn> in Peking (.) University, .hh we just saw a yellow mass.'

04 TIN: → [很 漂 -
[hen piao-
very beautiful
'Very beauti-'

05 (.)

---

[17] Although no details are offered about how they began to have mangosteen and it is also possible that the story recipient's action (disagreement) influences the shape of the story, the second part (lines 18-19) still appears as a continuation of the first part (lines 2-4) along the development of the story's temporal line. Actually, what the storyteller tells is always selective, and motivated by many factors, e.g. the purpose of the storytelling, the time limit of telling a story, or the recipient. Thus, storytelling is a rather open activity, and the storyline is also adjusted contingent on how the interaction unfolds.

06 LEN: 很 ci- 很 si- (.) 很 丑:.=
hen ci- hen si- (.) hen chou:.=
very very very ugly
'Very ci- very si- (.) very ugly.'

07 TIN: =很 丑 :: 啊 .=
= hen chou:: a.=
very ugly PRT
'=Very ugly.= '

08 LEN: =黄: 的 草坪, =不 好看 呐 秋天 .
= huang: de caoping, = bu haokang na qiutian.
yellow PRT lawn no good-looking PRT autumn
'=Ye:llow lawn,=not good-looking in Autumn.'

09 (0.4)

10 TIN: 哦 :::[:
'O :::[:'

11 LEN: → [然后 那个 北京 的 那个 香山 (xx-)
[ranhou nage Beijing de nage xiangshan (xx-)
then that-CL Bei.Jing PRT that-CL Fragrant.Hills
'And then the Fragrant Hills in Beijing (xx-)'

Here, Lena's telling is about the photos of the autumn scene on campus of Peking University sent from the friend (lines 1-3). Her telling gets halted by the side sequence initiated by Tina who gives a predictive assessment that the photo must look very beautiful (line 4). Responding to Tina's 'very beauti-' (line 4), Lena's utterance 'Very ci- very si- (.) very ugly' (line 6) shows Tina that her predictive assessment is just the opposite of the kind of assessment intended by her. This side sequence then expands when Tina acknowledges with 'Very ugly' (line 7) and Lena further explains that 'Ye:llow lawn,=not good-looking in Autumn' (line 8). After Tina produces the utterance 'o::::' (line 10), which appears to be a receipt token to the storyteller's explanation in line 8, Lena continues 'And then the Fragrant Hills in Beijing (xx-)' (line 11). This switch of topic shows that she is returning to her telling about the photos of different locations in Beijing sent by her friend (lines 1-3).

Recall that at the beginning of the story, Lena's mention of asking her friend to take photos of different locations of Beijing projects a telling of a list of photos from various places. With this background, Lena's telling about the Fragrant Hills in Beijing (line 11) can be heard as a continuation onto the next item on the list following her recount of the photo showing the lawn at Peking University. That is, the utterance following the side sequence picks up from a new component from the storyteller's projected list of photos of different locations in Beijing (among which the lawn in Peking University is the first one). If we look at Lena's telling before and after the side sequence it is clear that the returning here is achieved through a direct continuation to a new item (the Fragrant Hills) in the story. The pick-up from prior telling proceeds as if there had been no interruption.

(5-07b)

01 LEN: .h 他 有 一次 给 我们 寄来 那个 (.) 北 (.) 大
.h ta you yici gei women ji-lai nage (.) bei(.) da
he have one.time to us mail-COMP that-CL Peking.U

02 的 那个 z-(.) < 秋天 的 草坪 >, .hh 就 看到
de nage z-(.) <qiutian de caoping>, .hh jiu kan-dao
PRT that-CL autumn PRT lawn just see-COMP

03 黄压 [压 的 .
huangya[ya de.
yellow.mass PRT
'.h Once he sent us the photo of <the lawn in Autumn> in Peking (.) University, .hh we just saw a yellow mass.

…… ((omitted side sequence, 7 lines))

11 LEN: → [然后 那个 北京 的 那个 [香山 (xx-)
[ranhou nage Beijing de nage [xiangshan (xx-)
then that-CL Bei.Jing PRT that-CL Fragrant.Hills
'And then the Fragrant Hills in Beijing (xx-)'

Taken together, these examples (5-05, 5-06, and 5-07) show that returning to prior telling can be accomplished by directly tying back to the point at which the story gets suspended by side sequence. The storyteller may return to prior telling by direct continuation as exemplified in cases where she adds more details to the story-so-far (5-05), recounts the next event along the temporal line (5-06), or produces the next story element in the projected listing (5-07). These returnings are performed as though there had been no intervening sequence that once suspended the telling. In all these cases, *ranhou* 'and then' is used as a continuation initiator, but in slight different ways. The continuation initiated with *ranhou* 'and then' in extract (5-06) shows a direct temporal relation between the continuation and the halted storytelling, i.e. the linear arrangement of the telling coincides with the temporal sequence of the events being recounted. In this case *ranhou* 'and then' can be seen as doing a double job as a temporal connective and a discourse marker. In contrast, the continuations in extracts (5-05) and (5-07) do not explicitly reveal a temporal relation to prior telling. *Ranhou* 'and then' in these cases mainly functions as a discourse marker which indicates the linear arrangement of the telling. The analysis presented in this section shows that storytellers may return to prior telling through direct continuation. At the close of the side sequence the teller may proceed with the next component in the telling as if there had been no interruption. Direct continuation is often prefaced with the discourse marker *ranhou* ('and then') which, developed from being a temporal connective, takes on the interactional function in signaling the continuation along the linear arrangement of the telling.

5.2.3 Pre-indication of an imminent return

As we have seen, returning to prior telling can be signaled by a repetition of a portion of the interrupted story or by a direct continuation of the halted telling. In addition, the storyteller may pre-indicate an upcoming return when still in the side sequence. By showing her attempt to close the ongoing side sequence, the storyteller can take the advantage of being the speaker of the current turn to achieve a return. My analysis of the data shows that tellers often use *fanzhen* 'anyway' in pre-indicating an imminent return.

Fanzheng 'anyway' in Chinese serves various adverbial functions (Lü, 1980). It can emphasize the inflexibility or certainty of a conclusion, e.g. *Xinbuxin you ni,* fanzheng *wo buxin* 'Believe it or not, anyway I don't believe it', or it can indicate a situation or reason for an event with a strong affect, e.g. Fanzheng *buyuan, zanmen jiu zou zhe qu ba!* 'Anyway it's not far away, let's walk there!' (Lü, 1980, p. 199-200). In addition, *fanzheng* 'anyway' may also be used as a discourse marker that prefaces concluding remarks (Dong, 2008). That is, a sense of concluding is indicated.

Fanzheng 'anyway' in spoken discourse may also be used to introduce a compensation when the speaker acknowledges that his/her knowledge about the current subject is limited. The compensation introduced by *fanzheng* 'anyway' can be a piece of information which is relevant to the topic at issue. The following is an example. Just preceding the extract below (5-08), Amy has been explaining that some people in their school tried to lift the girls' skirts. Then Max asks a question about the security measures in Amy's school (line 1).

(5-08) SR_M11_2632_Public security

01 Max: >你们 学校 <你们 学校 治安 >不<会 好 一点 吗.
>nimen xuexiao < nimen xuexiao zhi'an > bu < hui hao yidian ma
your school your school security not will good a.bit Q
'>Your school< can't your school have better security measures.'

02 Amy: → 我 不 知道:, 反正, 都 不 是 我们 学校 自己
wo bu zhidao:, fanzheng, dou bu shi women xuexiao ziji
I not know anyway all not be our school self

03 的 人 嘛, 应该 是 外面 来 °的° .
de ren ma, yinggai shi waimian lai ° de° .
PRT people PRT maybe be outside come PRT
'I don't know:, anyway, they are not people from our school, they shoulde be outsiders.'

Orienting to Max's question, Amy first responds 'I don't know'. Following this acknowledgement of not knowing about the security issue, Amy uses *fanzheng* 'anyway' to introduce a piece of information she is sure about: those who tried to lift girls' skirts are not from their school but should be from outside. Although the 'I don't know' acknowledges that the storyteller may not be able to provide an exact answer to Max' question, the piece of information introduced by *fanzheng* 'anyway' offers compensation for Amy's not knowing.

In addition to this particular function, *fanzheng* 'anyway' often pre-indicates an impending resumption to prior telling. In the conversation below, the storyteller Su recounts the boring tour they had in Singapore and complains about the bad arrangement made by the tour agency. Prior to this extract, (5-09), reproduction of (4-08), the storyteller Su has been telling Yi that the tour agency did not take the tourists to have local food in Singapore, but only let them have Chinese food for breakfast.

(5-09) SR_M01_1518_Do cats eat watery things [storyteller = Su; recipient = Yi]

01 苏: 那些 中餐 啊,.h 好::[搞笑 就是,(0.8) 就是, =
Su: naxie zhongcan a, .h hao::[gaoxiao jiushi, (0.8) jiushi,=
those Chinese.food PRT very funny that.is that.is

02 易: [((咳嗽))((咳嗽))
Yi: *[((cough))((cough))*

03 苏: =它那个xi- 那个 粥: 很 稀 很 稀
Su: = ta nage xi- nage zhou: hen xi hen xi
it that-CL that-CL porridge very watery very watery

04 很 稀 嘛,.h 稀(h)到:(h) .h 最后 他们 就-.h
hen xi ma,.h xi (h) dao:(h) .h zuihou tamen jiu- .h
very watery PRT watery-COMP finally they just

05 >就是<有 一个 人 就是,其中 的 一个
> jiushi< you yige ren jiushi, qizhong de yige
that.is there.is one-CL person that.is among PRT one-CL

06 阿姨 就 说,(0.3)那-我们 那里 都 说 是 这 是
ayi jiu shuo,(0.3) na- women nali dou shuo shi zhe shi
auntie just say that we there all say be this be

07 喂 猫::吃 的 那(个/种) 猫:食 呢(xx)就是
wei mao:: chi de na (ge/zhong) mao:shi ne (xx) jiushi
feed cat eat PRT that(CL/type) cat.food PRT that.is

08 很 稀 很 稀 的[嘛.
hen xi hen xi de [ma.
very watery very watery PRT PRT
'That Chinese food,.h the funny thing was,(0.8)that is,= that porridge: was very very very watery,.h the porridge was so watery that.h finally one person, one of the aunties said,(0.3)'that- in our hometown people would say this is for cats, this is cat food, (xx) that was very very watery."

09 易: [猫:都 吃 稀 的 啊.=
Yi: [mao: dou chi xi de a.=
cat all eat watery PRT Q
'Do cats eat watery things.'

10 苏: =我 不 知(h)道(h),[他们 是 这样 形容 的,=
Su: = wo bu zhi(h)dao(h), [tamen shi zheyang xingrong de,=
I not know they be this-CL describe PRT
'=I don't know, they described it like this,='

11 易: [huh huh huh (.) huh .h
Yi: *[huh huh huh (.) huh .h*

12 苏 : → =.h 然后 反正 也 [不是 那么 很 好吃 啊 =
Su: =.h ranhou fanzheng ye [bushi name hen haochi a=
then anyway also not that very delicious PRT

13 易 : [((咳嗽))
Yi: *[((cough))*

14 苏 : =什么的 然后 后来 , .h 中午 我们 就 - 她 就
Su: = shenmede ranhou houlai, .h zhongwu women jiu- ta jiu
and.so.on then later noon we just she just

15 一开始 就 带 我们 去 : 一个 sh- 购物
yikaishi jiu dai women qu: yige sh- gouwu
in.the.beginning just bring us go one-CL shopping

16 的 地方 然后 , ((story continues))
de difang ranhou,
PRT place then
'=And anyway it didn't taste very good and then, .h at noon we just- in the very beginning she just brought us to a place for shopping and then,' ((story continues))

Extract (5-09) begins with the storyteller Su describing the kind of porridge they had for breakfast when travelling in Singapore. As the porridge was very watery (lines 3-4), one of the members in the tour group said that this kind of food was only given to cats in their hometown (lines 4-7). Su's telling is sidetracked at this point as Yi asks a question if cats eat watery things (line 9). Responding to Yi's question, Su first replies, 'I don't know' (line 10), and then explains that 'they described it like this' (line 10). As I have discussed in the previous chapter, the storyteller Su's ongoing storytelling gets halted when she begins to orient to Yi's question. After a brief explanation, Su adds 'and anyway it didn't taste very good' (line 12). Her next utterance, 'at noon we just- in the very beginning she just took us to a place for shopping' (line 14-16) is a direct return to the suspended story.

Focusing on the sequential position of *fanzheng* 'anyway', we can see that it occurs in a similar sequential position as in the previous example (5-08); in each case, the utterance 'I don't know' shows the storyteller's disclaim to the knowledge required for answering the question. The utterance introduced by Su's *fanzheng* 'anyway' (in line 12), 'it didn't taste very good', provides a piece of experiential information about the watery porridge. This piece of experiential information about the porridge compensates for Su's 'I don't know': although she does not know about the diet of cats, she knows about particular aspects of the watery porridge which did not have a good taste. At the same time, the *fanzheng* 'anyway'-prefaced utterance projects an impending ending of her response to the story recipient's question, therefore possibly indicating an upcoming return to the interrupted story. As shown in extract (5-09), Su's utterance in lines 14-16 shows she has returned to her story where the next component is what the tour group did at noon rather than staying on the topic of cat food. That is, the occurrence of *fanzheng* 'anyway' can be understood, to certain extent, as a pre-indicator of the return to the halted story, as it signals impending closure of the current talk.

The use of *fanzheng* as a pre-return marker is similar to the use of its English counterpart 'anyway'; previous studies have shown that 'anyway' can signal resumption of an interrupted activity or project (Koenig, 2005; Owen, 1985; Park, 2010⑱).

In the following example (5-10), the occurrence of *fanzheng* 'anyway' also indicates an intention to return to a suspended story, although the storytelling resumption is not achieved immediately. Prior to this extract, Ada has been telling Bes that one of her classmates is very talented but was unlucky, since he was stuck in a part-time job with a very low salary in his third year at university.

(5-10) SR_M18_2517_Blue cat [storyteller = Ada; recipient = Bes]

01 Ada: 然后 :, (.) 也 算 我们 老师 介绍 过去 的 嘛 .
ranhou:, (.) ye suan women laoshi jieshao guoqu de ma.
then also count our teacher introduce there PRT PRT

02 .hh 然后 刚 开始 , (.) 刚 开始 都 没 给 他
.hh ranhou gang kaishi, (.) gang kaishi dou mei gei ta
then just beginning just beginning even not give him

03 钱 , .hh 但是 刚 开始 只是 : 去 培训 他 : (.)
qian,.hh danshi gang kaishi zhishi: qu peixun ta: (.)
money but just beginning only go train him

⑱ Park's (2010) study is focused on the use of anyway as a "sequence-closing device". In the very beginning, she states that this is different from its use as a resumption marker. Unfortunately, however, she does not provide any literature describing this lexeme's use as a resumption marker.

04 就 做 那个 特效 . (0.4).h 然后 : [因为 他 -
jiu zuo nage texiao (0.4).h ranhou: [yinwei ta-
just make that-CL special.effect then because he
'And then:, (.) he's counted as a student introduced by our teacher. .hh and then in the very beginning, (.) in the very beginning they didn't give him money, .hh but in the very beginning it was to give him training only (.) just to make special effects. (0.4) .h And then: because he-'

05 Bes: [> 他 现在
[> ta xianzai
he now

06 做 的 好不好 <.
zuo de haobuhao<.
make PRT good-not-good
'Is he doing well now.'

07 (0.4)

08 Ada: 特 - 特别 好 , = 相当 > 好 <, 他 以前 在 学校 : 做
te- tebie hao,= xiangdang >hao<, ta yiqian zai xuexiao: zuo
very very good fairly good he before in school make

09 的 就 相当 好 ..hh 而且 他 参加 了 什么 :
de jiu xiangdang hao..hh erqie ta canjia le shenme:
PRT just fairly good and.also he join PRT something

10 (.).hh(.) 有 一部 新 上映 的 , 动画片
(.).hh(.) you yibu xin shangying de, donghuapian
there.is one-CL newly release PRT cartoon

11 叫 什么 蓝::: 猫 :::?=
jiao shenme lan:::mao:::?=
name something blue.cat
'Very- very good, = fairly >good<, when he was in school: he was doing fairly good. .hh And he also joined something: like (.).hh(.) there was a newly released video, a cartoon whose name is something like blue::: cat:::?='

12 Bes: = 虹兔 (.) 三千 问 .
=hongtu (.) sanqian wen.
rainbow.rabbit three.thousand question
'=Rainbow rabbit's (.) three thousand questions.'

13 (0.4)

14 Ada: 不是 .
bushi.
no
'No.'

15 Bes: huh huh huh
huh huh huh

16 (0.4)

17 Ada: 蓝猫 警长？ (.) 不是 . (0.4) 叫 - 叫 蓝猫 什么 .
lanmao jingzhang?(.) bushi. (0.4) jiao- jiao lanmao shenme.
blue.cat sheriff no name name blue.cat sth.

18 → (0.7) 反正 就 叫：>什么< 猫 什么， 然后 就
(0.7) fanzheng jiu jiao: >shenme< mao shenme, ranhou jiu
anyway just name sth. cat sth. then just

19 参加 了 那个 项目 嘛 . (0.9) 对 . (0.3) 就是：那个：
canjia le nage xiang-mu ma. (0.9) dui. (0.3) jiushi: nage:
join PRT that-CL project PRT right that.is that-CL

20 (0.4) 什么 猫 , (0.4) 然后 后来 他 就 辞职 ,= 他
(0.4) shenme mao,(0.4) ranhou houlai ta jiu cizhi, = ta
sth. cat then later he just resign he

21 今年 就 辞职 了 . ((story continues))
jinnian jiu cizhi le.
this.year just resign PRT
'Sheriff Blue Cat?(.)No.(0.4)Name- the name is something. (0.7)Anyway, its name is >something< cat something, and then he just joined that project.(0.9) Right.(0.3)that's: that: (0.4) something cat. (0.4) And then he just resigned, = he resigned this year.'

At the beginning of this extract, Ada says that when her classmate began his job, the company didn't pay him since he started there to get training in making special effects (lines 1-4). However, Ada's ongoing storytelling gets halted by a side sequence initiated by Bes's question on if the classmate is doing well now (lines 5-6). As it turns out, Ada's answer develops into a lengthy one during which she mentions that her classmate joined in the making of a cartoon movie but gets stuck at producing the title of the movie (lines 8-11). The sequence further develops when Bes comes in to help in the search of the title of the cartoon by proffering a candidate one (line 12). However, the joint search is not very successful after they have tried a couple of names.

At this point, Ada has been searching for the name of the cartoon for a relatively long time (lines 9-11 and 17) and Bes has also participated in helping with the search. Finally Ada produces the utterance prefaced by *fanzheng*, 'Anyway its name is

>something< cat something' (line 18), indicating this is the best she can do as a result of the search. Here, Ada displays her uncertain epistemic status about the question at issue (the exact name of the cartoon). By using *fanzheng* 'anyway', Ada also indicates she is giving up on the search and thus proposes to close the sequence on name search. Her subsequent utterance 'and then he just joined that project' (lines 18-19) shows that she is returning to the storytelling about how well her classmate is doing (lines 8-10). After a 0.9-second silence, Ada produces a *dui* 'right' utterance in line 19, and then affirms again 'that's: that: (0.4) something cat' (lines 19-20). Interestingly, Ada does not directly continue the story when she returns to the telling (lines 18-19). Rather, she first pauses to do a self-affirmation, although she still can't remember the name of that cartoon. After a 0.4-second pause, Ada's utterance 'and then he just resigned, = he resigned this year' (lines 20-21) shows that she has fully returned to the story about her classmate.

From (5-10), we can see that, the utterance prefaced with *fanzheng* 'anyway' signals the speaker's attempt to close on whatever is being talked about at the moment. Thus, in the case of recipient-initiated side sequence during an ongoing telling, the teller's *fanzheng* 'anyway'-prefaced utterance, while still in the side sequence, helps to manage its closure and project possible resumption. Whether the teller resumes earlier telling immediately after the *fanzheng* 'anyway'-prefaced utterance is a separate matter. The analytical point here is that storyteller can propose to close a sequence that has sidetracked his/her telling by a *fanzheng* 'anyway'-prefaced utterance in preparation for returning to prior telling.

5.2.4 Extra effort in managing returning

On certain occasions, a return to the prior halted telling can not be straightforwardly achieved through the practices described above. Rather, as contingencies occur, the storyteller often has to make an extra effort to go back to his/her previous telling. For instance, the storyteller may abort the possible continuation and restart from the beginning of the story; he/she may resist possible further expansion of the side sequence after being interrupted several times; he/she may also do a resuming search and attempt to tie back to a halted telling which occurred many turns earlier.

Prior to the extract below (5-11), Fen has told Lin and Wan that every time a French man met her friend Sister Shanxi, he would say that he loved Sister Shanxi, but

Sister Shanxi did not like that guy.

(5-11) SR_M09_1547_French drunkard [storyteller = Fen; recipient = Wan and Lin]

01 芬: >然后<, (0.8) 有 一天 晚上 四点钟 的 时候, =
Fen: >ranhou<,(0.8) you yitian wanshang si-dianzhong de shihou,=
then there.is one.day night four-o'clock PRT time
'>And then<, (0.8) once at four o'clock in the morning,='

02 琬: =mm
Wan: *=mm*

03 (.)

04 芬: 山西 姐姐, = 她们 那个 >寝室< 睡 了. (0.4)
Fen: shanxi jiejie,= tamen nage >qinshi< shui le. (0.4)
Shanxi sister they that-CL dorm sleep PRT

05 然后 他们 喝:醉 了,= 就 法国人 带 了
ranhou tamen he:zui le,= jiu faguoren dai le
then they drunk PRT that.is French bring PRT

06 一群: 人 回来,= 因为 我们 那个 就
yiqun: ren huilai,= yinwei women nage jiu
one-group people back because we that-CL that.is

07 纯: 公寓, =没 有 保安 的.
chun: gongyu, = mei you bao'an de.
pure apartment not have security.guard PRT
'Sister Shanxi, = people in their dorm were asleep.(0.4) And then they were drunk, = the French man brought a grou:p of people back, = because we were simple apartments, = we didn't have a security guard.'

08 琳: mm
Lin: *mm*

09 (0.4)

10 芬: 然后, (0.9)>就 在<那里 唱歌 啊 什么 喝醉 了,
Fen: ranhou, (0.9)>jiu zai< nali changge a shenme hezui le,
then just be there sing PRT and.so.on drunk PRT

11 =然后 去 踹 她们 门 哎.
=ranhou qu chuai tamen men ai.
then go kick their door PRT
'And then, (0.9) they were singing and so on and they were drunk, = and then they went to kick the girls' door.'

12 (0.3)

13 琳 : → m-[法国人 ,
Lin: m-[faguoren,
French
'm- the French man,'

14 芬 : [就 去 - [对的 , 就 (x)
Fen: [jiu qu- [duide, jiu (x)
just go right just
'Just went- yeah, just (x)'

15 琳 : [噢 你们的 是 - 也 是 男女混住
Lin: [ao nimende shi- ye shi nannvhunzhu
INT yours be also be gender-neutral.housing

16 的 [是吗 .
de [shima.
PRT Q
'Ao, are you- are you also having both boys and girls living together.'

17 芬 : [对的 ,= 就是 五个 人 一个 - (0.4) 五个 人
Fen: [duide,= jiushi wuge ren yige- (0.4) wuge ren
right that.is five-CL people one-CL five-CL people

18 两 : 个 洗手间 两个 厕所 . =
liang:ge xishoujian liangge cesuo.=
two-CL washroom two-CL toilet
'Yeah, = that is, five people have one- (0.4) five people have two washrooms and two toilets.='

⋯ ⋯ ((omitted sequence, 30 lines omitted, during which the story recipient continues to ask questions about the apartment, and the storyteller answers those questions.))

49 琳 : 那 [男的 肯定 也 -
Lin: na [nande kending ye-
that man must.be also
'That man must also be'

50 芬 : → [> 然后 -<
Fen: [>ranhou-<
then
'>And then-<'

51 (0.5)

52 琳：[° b- 会 告诉 他 哎呀 我 对 你 没 兴趣° .
Lin: [° b- hui gaosu ta aiya wo dui ni mei xingqu° .
would tell him INT I in you not interest
'°b- (Someone) would tell him, 'Aiya I'm not interested in you°.''

53 芬：[(那)个 法国 男的 半夜 四点 带着 一
Fen: [(na)ge faguo nande banye si-dian dai-zhe yi-
that-CL French man midnight four-o'clock bring-ASP one-

54 群 醉鬼 去 -(0.4) 去 sh- 打 -[开 她们的 门 哎，=
qun zuigui qu -(0.4) qu sh- da- [kai tamende men ai,=
group drunkard go go open open their door PRT
'That French man brought a group of drunkards at four o'clock in the midnight to- (0.4) to open- open their door,='

55 琳：[mm
Lin: *[mm*

56 芬：=[开 那 两个 女生 的 门，=[还 踹 她们的 门 .
Fen: =[kai na liangge nvsheng de men, = [hai chuai tamende men.
open that two-CL girl PRT door also kick their door
'(They) opened the two girls' door, = and also kicked their door.'

57 琳：[mm [mm
Lin: *[mm [mm*

58 (0.6)

59 芬：她 吓 :[: 死 了.=
Fen: ta xia :[:si le.=
she scare.to.death PRT
'She was scared to death.='

60 琳：[m-
Lin: *[m-*

61 琳：=醉 了 吧，= 应该 . (0.3) 以为 是 自 [己 的，= 哦 .
Lin: = zui le ba, = yinggai. (0.3) yiwei shi zi [ji de, = o.
drunk ASP PRT maybe think be own PRT INT
'=Got drunk, = maybe.(0.3) (They may) think it's theirs,=o.'

62 琬：[醉 了 .
Wan: [zui le.
drunk ASP
'Got drunk.'

63 芬：[她们 幸亏
Fen: [tamen xingkui
they luckily

64 锁 了 门，=我 跟 我 室友 从来 不 锁 门。=
suo le men,= wo gen wo shiyou conglai bu suo men.=
lock ASP door I with my roommate never not lock door
'It's very lucky that they locked the door, = my roommate and I never locked the door.'
((Fen continues to state the reason why they didn't lock the door.))

Extract (5-11) begins with the storyteller Fen's recounting about a time when a French man brought a group of drunk people back to the apartment in the middle of the night and kicked the door of her friend Sister Shanxi's dorm (lines 1-11). Fen's *jiu qu-* 'just went-' (line 14), which occurs in overlap with Lin's utterance in line 13, indicates the storyteller Fen's intention to continue the story. However, Fen's recount of what the Frenchman did next after kicking on the door of her friend's room is sidetracked by Lin's confirmation request (line 13). The side sequence then gets expanded following Fen's confirmation (line 14) when Lin asks a series of questions about the condition of that apartment (her first question is shown in lines 15-16). As shown in the extract, Fen tries to return to the halted storytelling when Lin's utterance at line 49 indicates she is still on the topic of a man in that apartment.

At lines 49 and 50, Lin and Fen almost start talking simultaneously. Lin's utterance 'That man must also be' (line 49), which is still about the man they discussed during the lengthy sequence (not the French guy), occurs a bit earlier than Fen's '>And then-<' (line 50). Here, Fen's '>And then-<' actually shows her attempt to return to her telling about what the Frenchman who was very rude to her friend. However, both Lin and Fen abort. After a 0.5-second silence (line 51), both of them simultaneously begin to talk again. Lin's utterance 'b- would tell him, I'm not interested in you' (line 52) is a continuation of what 'that man' (line 49) would do, and meanwhile Fen's utterance 'That French man brought a group of drunkards at four o'clock in the midnight to- (0.4) to open- open their door' (lines 53-54) is a restart of her story from line 1.

Fen's utterance in lines 53-56 shows a restart from the very beginning of her earlier story. First, the exact time reference ('four o'clock in the midnight', line 1) is re-introduced in line 53. Then the story characters ('the French man' and 'a group of people who are drunk', lines 5-6) are also re-introduced as '(that) French man brought a group of drunkards' in lines 53 and 54. Furthermore, the story event ('kicked the girls' door', line 11) is also re-introduced in line 56. Here, most of the re-introduction of the story components in line 52 (including the time reference, story characters, and story event) is delivered in a long overlapping with Lin's utterance in line 53, showing that Fen is persistent in getting back to her story which was started but not completed. As it is now a long distance from where the story was interrupted, what Fen does is not continuing from where she was interrupted but restarts from the very beginning of that story.

Back in line 50, Fen's *ranhou* 'and then' could be heard as signaling a return to the story, However, because Lin's utterance in line 49 overlaps with Fen's, Fen has to reattempt her story return. This time, she restarts the story, but she does not just continue from where her story was interrupted. Instead, because of the occurrence of the overlap, Fen makes an extra effort to ensure the storytelling return will be achieved.

In the next example (5-12), the storyteller makes a continuous effort to pull her own storytelling back from disruptive talk by the story recipient. Prior to the extract, another participant, Lin, has just finished a story about her friend's observation of people evading buying a ticket in the U.S.. At the beginning of the extract, Wan launches a possible story beginning. This occurs at 2min55sec of the recording.

(5-12) SR_M09_0255_Faredodger in Paris [storyteller = Wan; recipient = Fen and Lin]

01	琬： Wan:	我 - 我有 一天 在巴黎 地铁 那边 的 时候 wo- wo you yi-tian zai bali ditie na-bian de shihou I I there.is one-day in Paris subway that-side PRT time
02		等 人. deng ren. wait people *'I- I once stood in the Paris metro and waited for someone.'*
03		(1.0)
04	琬： Wan:	然后 就 看到 了 各种各样 在 巴黎 地铁 里面 ranhou jiu kan-dao le gezhonggeyang zai bali ditie limian then just see-COMP PRT various in Paris subway inside
05		逃票 的 方式 [° huh huh huh huh° taopiao de fangshi [° huh huh huh huh° evade.buying.ticket PRT way *'And then I saw various ways of evading buying tickets in the Paris subway °huh huh huh huh°'*

06 芬: → [我-上次 我 超::
Fen: [wo- shangci wo chao::
I last.time I super

07 生气. (0.3) 法国 >后头<我 在 西班牙 也 看 到-,
shengqi.(0.3) faguo >houtou< wo zai xibanya ye kan-dao
angry France later I in Spain also see-COMP
'I- last time I was super:: angry. (0.3) In France >later< in Spain I also saw it,'

((Fen continues her own story about faredodgers. At 4min17sec, her story reaches its completion, and then she makes a comment that compares people' s different attitudes toward faredodgers, as shown in line 9.))
…… ((omitted until 4min17sec))

08 芬: 他们 说 法国 超: 多 人 逃票, 然后
Fen: tamen shuo faguo chao: duo ren taopiao, ranhou
they say France super many people evade.buying.ticket then

09 如果 你 在 德国 逃票 别人 就 会
ruguo ni zai deguo taopiao bieren jiu hui
if you in Germany evade.buying.ticket other just would

10 鄙视 地 看 着 你.
bishi de kan zhe ni.
disdain PRT look PRT you
'They said that there are many faredodgers in France, but if you evade buying a ticket in Germany people will look at you disdainfully.'

11 (.)

12 琬: 法国 很 多 呀,=我 那天 就 大概 站 了 可能
Wan: faguo hen duo ya,= wo natian jiu dagai zhan le keneng
France very many PRT I that-day just about stand PRT maybe

13 三十 分钟 吧,=真的 是 看 到 了 各种各样
sanshi fenzhong ba,= zhende shi kan-dao le gezhonggeyang
thirty minute PRT really be see-COMP PRT various

14 [逃票 的 [方式.
[taopiao de [fangshi.
evade.buying.ticket PRT way
'In France there are many, = on that day I just stood there for about thirty minites, = really saw various ways of evading buying a ticket.'

15 芬: [我 在-
Fen: [wo zai-
I in
'I was in-'

16 琳: → [你 为什么 要 在 那里 站
Lin: [ni weishenme yao zai nali zhan
you why want in there stand

17 三 (h)[十 (h) >分钟 啊<.
san(h)[shi(h) > fenzhong a<.
thirty minute PRT
'Why did you stand there for thirty(h) >minutes<.'

18 琬: [因为 等 人, [(x)
Wan: [yinwei deng ren, [(x)
because wait people
'Because I was waiting for someone, (x)'

19 芬: → [我 在 [网上 看到 他们=
Fen: [wo zai [wangshang kandao tamen=
I in internet see-COMP they

20 琳: [mm:
Lin: *[mm:*

21 芬: =说 一个 老 太太 (.)t- 身手 特别 灵活 地
Fen: =shuo yi-ge lao taitai (.)t- shenshou tebie linghuo de
say one-CL old lady action very skillful PRT

22 就 从 那个 闸:那里 钻 过 [去 (h) huh huh [huh
jiu cong na-ge zha: nali zuan-guo[qu(h) huh huh [huh
just from that-CL gate there duck.through
'In the Internet I saw that they said one old lady (.) t- very skillfully ducked through(h) that gate huh huh huh'

23 琳: [hmh hmh hmh [hmh(.)=
Lin: *[hmh hmh hmh [hmh(.)=*

24 =hmh hmh hmh
=hmh hmh hmh

25 琬: [huh =
Wan: *[huh =*

26 → =huh huh 对, (.) 他们 有 从 底下 钻过去 的.=
=huh huh dui, (.) tamen you cong dixia zuan-guoqu de.=
right they have from under duck.through PRT
'huh huh huh Right,(.)they would duck through under it.'

27 琳: =mm=
Lin: *=mm=*

28 琬 : =有 从 上面 跳 过去 的 .(.) 然后 有
Wan: = you cong shangmian tiao guoqu de. (.) ranhou you
there.is from top jump over PRT then there.is

29 两个 人 一起 出 的 ,(.) 然后 有 那种
liang-ge ren yiqi chu de, (.) ranhou you na-zhong
two-CL person together exit PRT then there.is that-CL

30 有时候 有些 人 出来 他 推 着 那个 s- 婴儿
youshihou youxie ren chulai ta tui zhe na-ge s- ying'er
sometimes some people exit he push PRT that-CL baby.

31 琬 : 车， [或者 是 坐 [轮椅 的 .
Wan: che, [huozhe shi zuo [lunyi de.
carriage or be sit wheel.chair PRT
'Some of them jumped over. (.) And sometimes two people went out together, (.) and sometimes when people had a baby carriage, or a wheel chair.'

32 琳 : [mm
Lin: *[mm*

33 芬 : → [还 推 着 婴儿车
Fen: [hai tui zhe ying'erche
even push PRT baby.carriage

34 还 要 [逃票 .
hai yao [taopiao.
also want evade.buying ticket
'People also evaded even when they were with a baby carriage.'

35 琳 : [huh huh huh huh huh huh huh
Lin: *[huh huh huh huh huh huh huh*

36 琬 : → [> 不是 <.(.)> 听我说 吧 <,(.) 就 有 - 有些
Wan: [>bushi <.(.)> tingwoshuo ba <,(.) jiu you youxie
no listen.to.me PRT that.is some some

37 人 (.) 出来 的 时候 会 推 (.) 婴儿车 或 坐
ren (.) chulai de shihou hui tui(.) ying'erche huo zuo
people exit PRT time would push baby.carriage or sit

38 轮椅 然后 就 会 有 一个 专门 的 地方
lunyi ranhou jiu hui you yi-ge zhuanmen de difang
wheel.chair then just would have one-CL special PRT place

39 那个 地 -(.) 专门 就 它 宽 一点.
na-ge di- (.) zhuanmen jiu ta kuan yidian.
that-CL place special just it wide a.bit
'>No<. (.) >Listen to me<, (.) that is some- some people (.) when exiting with (.) a baby carriage or a wheel chair, there was a special place and that place- (.) was wider.'
((Wan continues to describe what she saw in the station.))

Extract (5-12) begins with Wan's recounting a time when she was standing in the Paris metro and witnessing various ways of evading buying tickets by some people (lines 1-5). This is a possible beginning of a storytelling in response to her co-participant's telling of a similar story (Faredodgers in the U.S.) a moment earlier. It also projects a telling which would instantiate what the 'various ways' are. However, this possible story beginning at 2min55sec does not get a 'go-ahead' signal from the other two co-participants, Fen and Lin. Rather, one of them, Fen, launches her own story of witnessing faredodgers in European countries (lines 6-7) with a strong affective display 'I was super:: angry.' At 4min17sec, Fen's story comes to a completion, and then she makes a comment about faredodgers in French and Germany (lines 8-10). Orienting to this comment, Wan first produces an utterance 'In France there are many' (line 12), affiliating with Fen's view that there are many faredodgers in France (line 8). Then, in lines 12-14, Wan re-begins (Sacks, 1995b) her story (lines 1-5) by saying 'on that day, I just stood there for about thirty minutes, = really saw various ways of evading buying a ticket.' As we can see, in lines 12-14, Wan uses 'on that day' to refer to the 'one day' in line 1, repeats the 'various ways of evading buying a ticket' from lines 4-5, and adds another specific time reference 'thirty minutes.' This time, after the re-beginning is launched, both Lin and Fen orient to Wan's story in lines 16-17 and lines 19-22, respectively.

Lin asks 'Why did you stand there for thirty(h) >minutes<' (lines 16-17), apparently picking this element in Wan's telling as remarkable and worth pursuing. Responding to Lin's question, Wan answers that she was waiting for someone (line 18). Fen, the other recipient also responds to Wan but she seems to be interested in another element in the story, i.e. Wan's mentioning that she saw various way of evading buying train tickets. To this, Fen responds by telling the story she read on the internet and relates how an old lady skillfully ducked through the ticket gate (lines 19, 21, and 22). Then, responding to Fen's telling of what she learned from the internet (lines 19-22), Wan first uses a *dui* 'right' utterance (line 26), then repeats the verb *zuan guoqu* 'duck through' which has been used by Fen in line 22, and another person reference *tamen* 'they' (in line 26). By doing this, Wan is able to take over the floor and successfully return to her previous storytelling. When Wan takes over she starts to give specific examples of various ways of evading buying train tickets she has witnessed in the subway station (lines 28-31), including someone pushing a baby carriage. Fen responds by 'even people with a baby carriage evaded buying ticket' (lines 33-34), which is produced in a playful way, revealing her slightly disdainful attitude toward the recounted behaviour in Wan's story. Fen's displaying of stance here could sidetrack Wan's telling if she chooses to respond to it. However, Wan produces the reply, '>No<. (.) >Listen to me<,' (line 36), explicitly resisting to go into a possible side sequence. After regaining the floor, Wan returns to her 'baby carriage' and 'wheel chair' reference (in line 37), and begins to elaborate on how people take advantage of the 'special' and 'wider ticket gate' (lines 38-39).

Recall that Wan's proposal of telling a story has not gone smoothly right from the beginning. First, at her announcement of having seen various ways of evading buying train tickets in Paris which projects an upcoming telling (liens 4-5), Fen jumps in with her own story of seeing people in other places evade buying train tickets. Then, when Wan gets back to her telling and projects the same telling a second time (lines 12-14), her telling does not materialize due to the side sequence initiated by Lin (lines 16-17) followed by Fen's story about the case she read on the internet (lines 19, 21-22). Now facing Fen's stance display in line 33, Wan risks losing tellership again. It is at this point that she explicitly shows her resistance. Her '>No<. (.) >Listen to me<,' (line 36) could be heard as competition for tellership. That is, her turn-initial 'no' is not produced to disaffiliate with Fen's disdainful stance, but is making an effort to take over the floor by demonstrating that she is entitled to do the telling. Furthermore, as Fen's utterance is produced and treated in a playful manner (mostly shown by the third participant Lin's laughter tokens in line 35), by using '>No<. (.) >Listen to me<,' (line 36), what the storyteller Wan does avoids the playful comment as well as permits her to become the focus of the current interaction (M. Goodwin, 1997). At the same time, this '>Listen to me<' is an "attention getter" that indicates "something that has been going on will now be re-attended" (Jefferson, 1972, p. 319). Thus, this resistance to a possible side sequence is an example of extra effort made on the part of the storyteller to accommodate the present story's particular sequential position and local contingencies.

In order to achieve a returning, the storyteller may also do a resumption search. Resumption search refers to the searching work a storyteller does before returning to telling per se. It usually occurs when both the storyteller and his/her co-participant agreed that the side sequence has come to an actual completion point. In addition, resumption search is not a single-handed activity done by the storyteller alone; the story recipient may also join in the search. That is, a resumption search not only signals the storyteller and recipient's readiness for the upcoming resumption but also prepares for the beginning of the returning. In doing the resumption search, the storyteller and recipient are negotiating where the previously ongoing storytelling got halted and where they should begin with the returning. Schegloff (2007) observes questions such as "where were we" can be used to indicate resumption search; he also observes that a resumption search is "a common occurrence after interruptions have run their course" (p. 24).

In the example below (5-13a), Su has been complaining about her mom's tour guide because the tour guide did not want Su to visit her mother. The background of this complaint is that Su was in Singapore as an intern and when her mother took a trip there on a tour Su wanted to take the opportunity to see her mother, for instance, to join their group for a day tour. Su has told Yi how she made a phone call with the tour guide, and the tour guide was still reluctant to let Su join their tour. The beginning of this extract occurs at 2min35sec into the recording.

(5-13a) SR_M01_0235_Where was I [storyteller = Su; recipient = Yi]

01	苏: Su:	我 说::, 那 你们: 今天 要 去 玩 哪 wo shuo::, na nimen: jintian yao qu wan na I say then you today want go travel which
02		几个 景点 我 去 哪 几- 那 几个: jige jingdian wo qu na ji- na jige: several scenery.spot I go which several that several-CL
03		来 找 你 就 好了 嘛 . .hh 然后 最后 她 lai zhao ni jiu haole ma. .hh ranhou zuihou ta come find you just ok PRT then finally she

04 就 说 :, >什么< 圣淘沙 鱼尾狮 公园
jiu shuo:, >shenme< shengtaosha yuweishi gongyuan
just say something Sentosa Merlion park

05 什么 什么 什 [么 ..h
shenme shenme shen[me .h
so.on.and.so.forth
'I said::, then today which scenery spots would you visit, I could go there to find you. .hh And then finally she just said: something like Sentosa the Merlion Park and so on.'

06 易 : → [话说 圣淘沙 是 什么 啊 ?
Yi: [huashuo shengtaosha shi shenme a?
as.to Sentosa be what Q
'Talking about Sentosa what is it?'

((Afterwards, Su and Yi continue to discuss Sentosa and the geographic location of Singapore. Later, Su begins to recount her experience at Universal Studios in the States and compares that with the one in Sentosa, Singapore. Yi also recalls that she saw a similar model in an exhibition in Hong Kong and recommends that Su go there.))

As analyzed in the previous chapter (see 4-20), Su's ongoing storytelling is suspended by the side sequence initiated by Yi's question about Sentosa. Subsequently, the side sequence develops into quite a lengthy one during which the chatting between the two friends goes from one topic to another. When the chat approaches 13min20sec in the recording, Su and Yi are talking about the dolls they played with when they were young. At the beginning of the following extract they are still on this topic.

(5-13b) SR_M01_0235_Where was I [storyteller = Su; recipient = Yi]

01 苏 : 你 妈 会 做 吗 ? huh huh
Su: ni ma hui zuo ma? huh huh
your mother can make Q
'Would your mother make the dresses? huh huh'

02 易 : 我 妈 :::: 不 知道 , >好像< 做 过 一两件 吧 .
Yi: wo ma:::: bu zhidao, >haoxiang< zuo guo yiliangjian ba.
my mother not know likely make ASP one-two-CL PRT
'My mother:::: I don't know, maybe she made one or two.'

03 (0.6)

04 苏: → ((headnod)) 好了，继续， 刚刚 我 讲 哪儿 了.
Su: ((headnod)) haole, jixu, ganggang wo jiang na'er le.
okay continue just.now I tell where PRT
'((head nod)) Okay, continue, where was I just now.'

05 (0.5)

06 苏: 哦:. [马来西亚 是不，
Su: o :. [malaixiya shibu,
oh Malaysia be-not
'Oh:. Was it Malaysia,'

07 易: [圣淘沙？
Yi: [shengtaosha?
Sentosa
'Sentosa?'

08 苏: 哦 圣淘沙:， >然后 我 就 -< 噢 - 哦 h 真的 扯
Su: o shengtaosha:, > ranhou wo jiu -< ao- o h zhende che
oh Sentosa then I just INTJ oh really chat

09 → 得 好 远 哦 .huh huh.hh 然后 我 就 说 好 吧？
de hao yuan o. huh huh.hh ranhou wo jiu shuo hao ba?
PRT very far PRT then I just say ok PRT

10 她 - 讲 的 那 几个 我 都 知道 在 哪里 嘛，
ta- jiang de na jige wo dou zhidao zai nali ma,
she say PRT that several-CL I all know in where PRT

11 然后 圣淘沙 我 就 q- 熟: 然后，.h 她 就 说
ranhou shengtaosha wo jiu q- shou: ranhou,.h ta jiu shuo
then Sentosa I just familiar then she just say

12 他们 吃 完 饭 之后 会 去 那里.
tamen chi wan fan zhihou hui qu nali.
they eat finish meal after would go there
'Oh Sentosa:, >and then I just-< ao- oh h we are really far away from where we were. huh huh .hh And then I just said ok? She- I know the places she mentioned, and I'm familiar: with Sentosa and then, she just said they would go there after having a meal.'

As Su is asking if Yi's mother made dresses for her dolls (line 1). Yi answers that she is not sure and maybe she made one or two (line 2). After this, there is no further talk on this topic, as evidenced by the 0.6-second gap in line 3. Then Su produces a head nod (indicated at the beginning of line 4) followed by the phrase *haole* 'okay', which is shift implicative (Miracle, 1989, 1991; Wang et al., 2010)[19]. Subsequently, Su's *jixu* 'continue' (in line 4) shows her plan to 'continue' on something other than the topic of dresses for dolls which has been closed by the shift-implicative *haole* 'okay'. Following *haole* 'okay' and *jixu* 'continue', Su is no doubt on resumption search when she produces the utterance *ganggang wo jiang na'er le* 'where was I just now' (line 4) This utterance shows she is trying to get back to a previously aborted activity. In this resumption search, the word *jiang* 'talk' indicates that this is a telling activity.

Furthermore, by indicating a resumption search, Su is also inviting Yi to help her in identifying the point where her telling got halted earlier. Her next utterance *malaixiya shibu* 'Is it Malaysia' (line 6) not only suggests Malaysia as a candidate point where she would resume with her telling, but also mobilizes the other speaker, Yi (shown in the turn final *shibu*), to ratify this suggested point for resumption. As it turns out, Yi responds to Su's resumption search in line 5, and suggests *shengtaosha* 'Sentosa' (line 7) as a candidate, overlapping with Su's 'is it Malaysia' (line 6).

On hearing Yi's candidate suggestion 'Sentosa' (line 7), Su realizes that Sentosa is the right point for resuming her telling, as evidenced by the change of state token *o* 'oh' followed by the repetition of 'Sentosa' in line 8, thus accepting Yi's suggested point for story resumption. Su's >*ranhou wo jiu-*< 'and then I just-' (line 8) is then momentarily put on hold by a parenthetical *zhende che de haoyuan* 'we are really far away from where we were' (lines 8-9), a comment made on how far they are from the original story (line 9). Then Su's *ranhou wojiu shuo hao ba* 'and then I just said ok' (line 9) shows that she is returning to her previous recounting about the phone call made with the tour guide in lines 1-5 in extract (5-13 a). That is, this utterance brings her back to where the story was interrupted.

To summarize, resumption search is used to manage a return to an interrupted story. Through the use of resumption search, the co-participant's collaboration can also be mobilized, and thus both the storyteller and recipient make efforts in searching for the point for return. At the same time, the two participants also prepare themselves to realign as storyteller and recipient again after a dramatically expanded side sequence.

---

⑲ Schegloff and Sacks (1973) also suggests "that one way to end a conversation is to present a pre-closing statement like we-ell, so-o-o, or okay, which signals a readiness to end the conversation" (cited in Wang et al., 2010, p. 253).

5.3 Interactional functions of storytelling return

This section analyzes the interactional functions served by returning to a previously halted storytelling. On certain occasions, returning to prior telling is made perhaps for the purpose of making the story complete and getting the point of the story across. In this case, the storyteller is dealing with the "incompleteness property" (Houtkoop and Mazeland, 1985, p. 599) of storytelling. On other occasions, a storyteller might return to a previously halted storytelling in order to complete the course of action that is carried by the story.

In the first two examples to be discussed in this section, after going back to the previously suspended telling, the storyteller is able to finish the story and give the gist of the original telling. Extract (5-11), reproduced below as (5-14), exemplifies this scenario. As was shown earlier in this chapter, Fen's telling in this extract about a rude French man is suspended in line 11, and she spends much effort in returning to her telling until she succeeds much later in their chat as shown from line 50 onwards.

(5-14) SR_M09_1547_French drunkard [storyteller = Fen; recipient = Wan and Lin]

01	芬 : Fen:	> 然后 <, (0.8) 有 一天 晚上 四点钟 的 时候 , = > ranhou<,(0.8) you yitian wanshang si-dianzhong de shihou,= then there.is one.day night four-o'clock PRT time *'>And then<, (0.8) once at four o'clock in the morning,='*
02	琬 : Wan:	=mm *=mm*
03		(.)
04	芬 : Fen:	山西 姐姐 ,= 她们 那个 > 寝室 < 睡 了 . (0.4) shanxi jiejie,= tamen nage >qinshi< shui le. (0.4) Shanxi sister they that-CL dorm sleep PRT
05		然后 他们 喝 : 醉 了, = 就 法国人 带 了 ranhou tamen he:zui le, = jiu faguoren dai le then they drunk PRT that.is French bring PRT
06		一群 : 人 回来 ,= 因为 我们 那个 就 yiqun: ren huilai,= yinwei women nage jiu one-group people back because we that-CL that.is

07 纯：公寓，=没有 保安 的.
chun: gongyu, = mei you bao'an de.
pure apartment not have security.guard PRT
'Sister Shanxi, = people in their dorm were asleep.(0.4) And then they were drunk, = the French man brought a grou:p of people back, = because we were simple apartments, = we didn't have a security guard.'

08 琳： mm
Lin: *mm*

09 (0.4)

10 芬： 然后，(0.9)> 就 在 <那里 唱歌 啊 什么 喝醉 了，
Fen: ranhou, (0.9)>jiu zai< nali changge a shenme hezui le,
then just be there sing PRT and.so.on drunk PRT

11 =然后 去 踹 她们 门 哎.
= ranhou qu chuai tamen men ai.
then go kick their door PRT
'And then, (0.9) they were singing and so on and they were drunk, = and then they went to kick the girls' door.'

…… ((omitted side sequence, 37 lines omitted))

49 琳： 那 [男的 肯定 也-
Lin: na [nande kending ye-
that man must.be also
'That man must also be'

50 芬： → [> 然后 -<
Fen: [>ranhou-<
then
'>And then-<'

51 (0.5)

52 琳： [° b- 会 告诉 他 哎呀 我 对 你 没 兴趣° .
Lin: [° b- hui gaosu ta aiya wo dui ni mei xingqu° .
would tell him INT I in you not interest
'°b- (Someone) would tell him, 'Aiya I'm not interested in you°.''

53 芬： [(那)个 法国 男的 半夜 四点 带着 一
Fen: [(na) ge faguo nande banye si-dian dai-zhe yi-
that-CL French man midnight four-o'clock bring-ASP one-

54 群 醉鬼 去 -(0.4) 去 sh- 打 - [开 她们的 门 哎，=
qun zuigui qu-(0.4) qu sh- da- [kai tamende men ai,=
group drunkard go go open open their door PRT
'That French man brought a group of drunkards at four o'clock in the midnight to- (0.4) to open- open their door,='

55 琳: [mm
Lin: *[mm*

56 芬: =[开 那 两个 女生 的 门, = [还 踹 她们的 门.
Fen: =[kai na liangge nvsheng de men, = [hai chuai tamende men.
open that two-CL girl PRT door also kick their door
'(They) opened the two girls' door, = and also kicked their door.'

57 琳: [mm [mm
Lin: *[mm* *[mm*

58 (0.6)

59 芬: 她 吓:[: 死 了.=
Fen: ta xia:[:si le.=
she scare.to.death PRT
'She was scared to death.='

60 琳: [m-
Lin: *[m-*

61 琳: = 醉 了 吧, = 应该. (0.3) 以为 是 自[己 的, = 哦.
Lin: = zui le ba, = yinggai.(0.3) yiwei shi zi [ji de, = o.
drunk ASP PRT maybe think be own PRT INT
'=Got drunk, = maybe.(0.3) (They may) think it's theirs,=o.'

62 琬: [醉 了.
Wan: [zui le.
drunk ASP
'Got drunk.'

63 芬: [她们 幸亏
Fen: [tamen xingkui
they luckily

64 锁 了 门, = 我 跟 我 室友 从来 不 锁 门.=
suo le men,= wo gen wo shiyou conglai bu suo men.=
lock ASP door I with my roommate never not lock door
'It's very lucky that they locked the door, = my roommate and I never locked the door.'
((Fen continues to state the reason why they didn't lock the door.))

In the initial telling, Fen's story is interrupted while her telling is about a group of drunk guys who went to kick the door of her friend Sister Shanxi (at line 11). After she restarts the story in lines 53-54 and 56, she continues with telling that her friend was extremely scared (line 59) because of the drunk men kicking at her door, but luckily they had locked their door (lines 63-64). At this point, when Fen points out that it's very lucky that the girls locked the door, she finally arrives at the high point of the story: although those men were drunk and kicked at the door of the girls' room, they were not harmed thanks to the locked door, because she herself and her flatmate were not in the habit of locking their door. Should Fen give up on getting back to the telling and bringing the story to completion, she would not be able to bring out the moral of the story which is usually better appreciated at the end of a story.

Similar to (5-14), (5-15) also shows a returning to the previous makes it possible for the storyteller to articulate the point of the story. The background of the extract is that Bes was admitted to the same college of her friend who is already a student. At this point in conversation Bes is talking about her college life at Ada's request. The extract begins with Bes' answer to Ada's inquiry about her first day to the college.

(5-15) SR_M18_0200_Go to school by oneself [storyteller = Bes; recipient = Ada]

01 Bes: 我 自-(.) 我 自：自己 一个 人 去：去 学校， (0.4)
wo zi- (.) wo zi: ziji yi-ge ren qu: qu xuexiao, (0.4)
I self I self self one-CL person go go school

02 → 然后，(.) 本来 - 本来 是 叫：(.) 本来 是
ranhou,(.) benlai- benlai shi jiao: (.) benlai shi
then originally originally be ask originaly be

03 叫 瑰 去 接 我 的.
jiao gui qu jie wo de.
ask Gui go pick.up me PRT
'I myself- (.) I went to school by myself, (0.4) and then, (.) at first- at first I was going to ask (.) at first I was going to ask Gui to pick me up.'

04 (.)

05 Ada: 你 [不 叫 你 妈妈 送 你 吗？
ni [bu jiao ni mama song ni ma?
you not ask your mother send.off you Q
'Didn't you ask your mother to send you off?'

06 Bes: [° 然后 -°
[° ranhou-°
then
'°And then-°'

…… ((omitted side sequence, 43 lines omitted))

50 Bes: → 本来 是 叫 瑰 去 接 我 的，[.h 然后 :=
benlai shi jiao gui qu jie wo de, [.h ranhou:
originally be ask Gui go pick.up me PRT then
'I was going to ask Gui to pick me up, .h and then ='

51 Ada: [° 嗯°
[°en°

52 Bes: => 我 就 说 <(.) Tch(.) 不 跟 她 说 :: 我 考 了
=> wo jiu shuo<(.) Tch(.) bu gen ta shuo:: wo kao le
I just say not to her say I be.admitted PRT

53 这个 学校， [(.)> 我 就 < 说 去 : eh: 她 肯定 =
zhe-ge xuexiao, [(.)>wo jiu< shuo qu: eh: ta kending=
this-CL school I just say go she must.be
'=>I just said< (.) Tch (.) I wouldn't tell her that I was admitted by this school, (.) I >just< said she must be ='

54 Ada: [huh
[huh

55 Bes: => 我 说 < .hh 我们 开学 的 时候 肯定 她 也
=>wo shuo< .hh women kaixue de shihou kending ta ye
I say we school.begin PRT time must.be she also

56 开学 啦，
kaixue la,
school.begin PRT
'=>I said< .hh when we began to go to school she must go to school too,'

57 Ada: ° 嗯°
° en°

58 Bes: 然后 就 给 她 打 个 电话， (0.3) 我 在 - 我 在
ranhou jiu gei ta da ge dianhua, (0.3) wo zai- wo zai
then just to her call CL telephone I at I at

59 学校 的 时候 就 给 她 打 了 个 电话 我
xuexiao de shihou jiu gei ta da le ge dianhua wo
school PRT time just to her call ASP CL telephone I

60 说，(.) 我 现在 在 学校 了 你 在 哪里 啦？
shuo,(.)wo xianzai zai xuexiao le ni zai nali la?
say I now at school ASP you at where Q

61 然后 她 说 (.) 我 在 家 里面，= 我 就 疯 - (0.3)
ranhou ta shuo (.) wo zai jia limian, = wo jiu feng- (0.3)
then she say I at home inside I then crazy

62 我 就 晕 了 (.) huh huh huh .h h .h h huh
wo jiu yun le (.) huh huh huh .h h .h h huh
I then mad PRT
'And then I called her,(0.3)when I was- I was at school I called her and I said,(.)'I'm at school now and where are you?' And then she said(.)'I'm at home,'=I then went crazy- (0.3) I was mad (.)huh huh huh .h h .h h huh'

Bes tells Ada that she went to the college by herself, although she had intended to ask her friend, Gui who is already a student there to meet her at the college (lines 1-3). However, Bes' telling is interrupted by another question from Ada asking why Bes did not ask her mother to take her to the college (line 5). Although Bes makes an attempt to continue her story with *ranhou* 'and then' at line 6, the attempt is aborted as it overlaps with Ada's question. Ada's second question results in a lengthy side sequence (not shown in the extract) during which the story just begun by Bes remains suspended.

Then at line 50 Bes' utterance 'and then at first I was going to ask Gui to meet me at the college' is a repetition of her previous utterance in lines 2-3, indicating that she is returning to the story. Now as Bes returns to it, she continues onto the next component in the story. She tells Ada that she planned not to inform her friend ahead of time about her admission to the same college (lines 52-53). She was pretty sure that when she arrived at the college her friend must be there as the new semester started (lines 53-56). Unfortunately, it turns out that when Bes called her friend from the college when she arrived there, her friend was actually at home (lines 58-61) so she got very crazy about it (line 62).

Here, it is hinted in the very beginning of the story when Bes says 'I was going to ask Gui to pick me up' (lines 2-3) that the actual event might have developed differently or there might be a change of the original plan. But Bes was not able to report how things actually turned out for the duration of the lengthy side sequence. When Bes finally returns to her story after line 50, she reveals that her plan did not work out as her friend Gui was not at school so she could not meet her on campus as a new fellow student. The climax comes near the end of the story when Bes wanted to surprise Gui by showing herself on campus of the college only to find Gui was still at home. She went crazy because the planned surprise fell flat. Should Bes not return to her story, what it amounts to would not materialize and the drama of the reported event would not be appreciated.

As reviewed in Chapter 2, stories can be told in order to implement certain courses of action. In this case, a return to a previously halted story may be undertaken in order to continue the course of action that was put on hold as the story was put on hold. That is, in certain cases where the course of action can be seen in the beginning, the returning is used to continue that action.

In the example below (5-16), the two graduate students have been talking about the distance between each other's home and school when they were undergraduates. Before the start of the extract, one of the participants, Yuan, has mentioned that some of his classmates had to stand in crowded trains when going home for the Chinese New Year. When Jiang announces 'I have this experience' at line 1, she is relating to the experience of those students described by Yuan. It projects a telling of similar experience of Jiang herself.

(5-16) ES_M06_0621_Impression [storyteller = Jiang; recipient = Yuan]

01	姜 : Jiang		我 : 有 :: 这个 经历 , = 我 就是 : 在 :: 北京 :: (.) wo: you:: zhege jingli, = wo jiushi: zai:: beijing::(.) I have this-CL experience I that.is in Bei.Jing
02			读 研究生 以后 [嘛 ,= 回家 可 : 难 了 . .hh du yanjiusheng yihou [ma,= huijia ke: nan le. .hh study master after PRT go.home very difficult PRT *'I: ha::d this experience, = after I began my Master's study in Beijing, = it was so: difficult to go home. .hh'*
03	袁 : Yuan		[mm *[mm*
04	姜 : Jiang		我 有 一次 是 从 :: 从 - (.) 兴国 那 > 个 < 时候 :, wo you yici shi cong:: cong-(.) xingguo na-> ge < shihou I there.is one-time be from from Xing.Guo that-CL time
05		→	火车 还 二十 s: 四 - (0.4) [个 ::(.) 多 小时 嘛 :. huoche hai ershi s: si- (0.4) [ge::(.) duo xiaoshi ma:. train still twenty four CL more hour PRT *'Once I started from:: from- (.) Xing Guo at that time:, by train it still took twenty f: four- (0.3) hours.'*

…… ((omitted side sequence, 6 lines omitted))

12 姜: → =对 对 对 .hhh 我 就是 - 我 也 是 .hh 一直
Jiang =dui dui dui .hhh wo jiushi- wo ye shi .hh yizhi
right right right I that.is I also be all.the.way

13 站 了 :: (0.3) 十 :: 七八个 小时 站 到
zhan le :: (0.3) shi :: qiba-ge xiaoshi zhan-dao
stand PRT seventeen.or.eighteen-CL hour stand-COMP

14 北京: (.) 非常 痛苦.
beijing: (.) feichang tongku.
Bei.Jing very painful
'Right right right .hhh I that is- I also .hh stood all the way (0.3) for about seventeen or eighteen hours to Beijing: (.) it's so painful.'

Then, when Jiang says 'after I began my Master's study in Beijing, = it was so difficult to go home' (lines 1-2), she is characterizing her experience of going home from Beijing as a very difficult one. Subsequently, in line 4, Jiang launches her story about a time when she took the trip to Beijing from Xing Guo, her hometown. As revealed in her telling the train ride would take her about twenty-four hours (lines 4-5); then her telling is sidetracked. Her story about the train ride as told up to this point appears to be incomplete, as the 'difficulty' has not been explicitly shown yet.

At the end of the side sequence (for about 6 lines), Jiang returns to her story by the utterance 'I that is- I also stood all the way (0.3) for about seventeen or eighteen hours to get to Beijing' (lines 12-14) after which she makes the assessment 'it's so painful' (line 14), echoing her earlier characterization of the trips between home and school: 'it was so difficult to go home' (line 2). By returning to the story, Jiang can complete the action carried through the story — substantiating the difficulty of going home — which was explicitly shown and projected at the story's beginning (lines 1 and 2). That is, by pursuing the 'completeness' of the story, the storyteller can fulfil what is projected at story beginning by giving a concrete instance from her own experience.

In the example below (5-17, a reproduction of 5-03), Lena's story is begun with the purpose of backing up her view that it was very hot when they travelled in Beijing in August. At this stage in the conversation, she has been arguing with Tina over the summer weather in Beijing. Tina thinks that in the evening it should not be too hot, but Lena argues that when they stayed in her friends' dorm it was very hot even in the evening. As with the last example, this story is told to substantiate the storyteller's view.

(5-17) ES_M11_0918_No power supply [storyteller = Lena; recipient = Tina]

01 LEN: 然后 :- (0.4) 她 - 我 不 知道 我 同学 她们 都 睡
ranhou:-(0.4) ta- wo bu zhidao wo tongxue tamen dou shui
then she I not know my classmate they all sleep

02 得 很 好 . (0.3).h 我 [妈 :: 她 也 睡 得 很 好 .
de hen hao.(0.3).h wo [ma :: ta ye shui de hen hao.
PRT very good my mother she also sleep PRT very good
'And the:n- (0.4) she- I don't know how come my classmates slept so well. (0.3).h My mother also slept very well.'

03 TIN: [你 还 : 觉得 很 热 .
[ni hai: juede hen re
you still feel very hot
'You sti:ll felt very hot.'

04 LEN: .hh 而且 他们 晚上 是 没 有 电 的 嘛 .=
.hh erqie tamen wanshang shi mei you dian de ma.=
and.also they night be not have electricity PRT PRT
'.hh And they didn't have power supply at night.='

…… ((omitted side sequence, 10 lines omitted))

15 LEN: → .hh 就是 限 - (.) 就 没 有 电 了 . =
.hh jiushi xian- (.) jiu mei you dian le. =
that.is restrict that.is no have electricity PRT
'.hh That's the restrict- (.) that's no power supply.='

16 TIN: =.hhh[(好) 惨 (呐).
=.hhh[(hao) can (na).
very tragic PRT
'=.hhh So tragic.'

17 LEN: [然后 - 我 一个 人 很 热 .(0.3) 然后 我 就
[ranhou- wo yige ren hen re. (0.3) ranhou wo jiu
then I one-CL person very hot then I just

18 去 把 他们 那 - 外面 那个 (.) 外面 那 块
qu ba tamen na- waimian nage (.) waimian na-kuai
go BA their that outside that-CL outside that-piece

19 走廊 的 一块 地方 s- (0.7) 扫扫 干 (h) 净 (h),
zoulang de yi-kuai difang s- (0.7) saosao gan(h)jing(h),
corridor PRT one-piece place sweep clean

20 [(0.4)] [铺 上 报纸 铺 张 席子 .]
[(0.4)] [pu-shang baozhi pu zhang xizi.]
spread-COMP newspaper spread CL mat
'And then- I myself felt very hot. (0.3) And then I just went out of the dorm and s- swept a place in the corridor,(0.4) spread a piece of newspaper and one mat.'

21 TIN: [huh huh] [< 躺 在 地上 >] =
[huh huh] [< tang zai dishang >] =
lie on ground
'huh huh Lying on the ground'=

22 LEN: = 对 .hh 然后 : (.) 就 睡 在 地 (h) 上 (h) .h 太 热 了 .
= dui .hh ranhou: (.) jiu shui zai di (h) shang(h).h tai re le.
right then just sleep on ground too hot PRT
'= Right .hh and then (.) just slept on the ground(h) .h It's too hot.' ((story continues))

As analyzed in Section 5.2.1, Lena's telling about lack of power supply (line 4) leads to a side sequence that suspends the progression of the story. At this point, her attempt to substantiate her point of view (that it was very hot at night in Beijing) is also put on hold.

Then Lena's utterance at line 15, which is a repetition of her last statement before the side sequence, identifies her return to the previously halted story. When she completes the repetition and resumes the telling, the course of action that is being carried through the story is also resumed/continued. Lena goes into a detailed telling about how she found a spot in the corridor, cleaned it up, and laid newspapers and a mat there for her to sleep on (lines 17-20, 22). This description of her experience explicitly supports her contention that it was very hot at night in Beijing in her argument with Tina.

Similar to extract (5-16), the return to the previous telling in this extract not only shows the storyteller's attempt to complete the story, but also shows her intention to implement her original course of action, which was put on hold by the side sequence.

5.4 Summary

In this chapter, I investigated the practices employed by storytellers in returning to a halted telling, presented my findings, and discussed the interactional functions that such returnings may serve. First, the data shows that a number of strategies are recurrently used by storytellers in returning to halted telling. For instance, the storyteller may repeat part of what was said in the telling before the occurrence of the side sequence as exemplified in 5-02, 5-03, and 5-04. The repetition can be done in several ways: the storyteller can repeat several story elements (extract 5-02), can repeat just the discourse marker *ranhou* 'and then' (extract 5-04), or can manipulate the closure of the side sequence as a repetition of one told story element (extract 5-03). My analysis shows that storytellers make their choices of the extent of the repetition based on the point at which the interruption occurred as well as other local contingencies.

The storyteller may also directly tie back to a halted telling without repetition, carrying on with the story as if no suspension had happened. A pervasive lexical choice for such direct continuation is the discourse marker *ranhou* 'and then', which as a temporal conjunction has developed into a discourse marker. It may perform dual functions as in some cases (as exemplified in 5-06) when the connection between the last part in the interrupted story and the first part in the resumed story have a temporal relation, and the linear arrangement of the telling coincides with the temporal relation of the events being recounted. In other cases, *ranhou* 'and then' is mainly used to organize the linear arrangement of the telling, showing more is to come in the telling, when there is no apparent temporal relation between the event in the interrupted story and when it is resumed. Extracts (5-05) and (5-07) are two examples that exemplify such use of *ranhou* 'and then'.

Whereas *ranhou* can serve to mark direct continuation, the use of *fanzheng* 'anyway' often pre-indicates an imminent return. This has to do with the general function of *fanzheng* which often proposes a close on whatever is being talked about. In this regard, the *fanzheng*-prefaced utterance by the storyteller while still in the side sequence is heard as proposing to close it, as exemplified in (5-09) and (5-10).

The current data also shows that sometimes a return can only be achieved through extra effort by the storyteller. Extracts (5-11), (5-12), and (5-13) reveal various special efforts made by the storyteller in order to manage a return to the halted story. For example, in extract (5-12), the storyteller resists a possible side sequence to compete for tellership after having been blocked twice from continuing her story; in extract (5-13), the storyteller initiates a resuming search after a rather lengthy side sequence. The question-formatted resuming search such as *wo gangcai jiangdao na'er le* 'where was I' also mobilizes the story recipient to participate in the search for a collaboratively achieved story return.

This chapter also examined possible interactional functions of achieving a story return. My analysis reveals that some returnings are motivated for the completeness of the telling in order to reach the moral and climax of the story, as exemplified in (5-14) and (5-15). However, if the initial story was launched in order to implement other actions in interaction (for instance, to substantiate a claim, stance, etc.), the interactional goal of the returning is to bring that course of action to completion in addition to bring the story itself to completion, as exemplified in (5-16) and (5-17).

In the next chapter, all the findings and implications of this study will be summarized and discussed.

Chapter 6

Conclusion

This book has examined two related phenomena in conversational storytelling — side sequence and story return — with a goal to explore how the storyteller and recipient co-organize the storytelling activity in Chinese conversation. I investigated in detail a collection of over one hundred storytelling sequences; each sequence was analyzed to see how the emergent storytelling was organized once it is begun. I investigated particular two phenomena in the telling sequence: (1) the organization of side sequences, i.e. breaks from the story occasioned by non-minimal responses on the part of the story recipient and the social actions implemented through those side sequences; (2) the recurrent practices adopted by the storyteller to effect a return to a halted telling and possible interactional functions such a return serves. In this concluding chapter, section 6.1 offers a summary and a discussion of implications of the preceding chapters. In section 6.2, the contribution of this study is discussed. In section 6.3 the limitations of the study are discussed, and directions for future study are suggested in section 6.4.

6.1 Summary and implications

Chapter 1 introduced the research topic of the current study. It sets the background of the research by a brief survey of studies on storytelling in various disciplines including CA. The aims and the rationale of the two focuses of the current study were also explained.

Chapter 2 presented a review of previous studies on storytelling from CA's perspective. Section 2.2 first discussed a number of techinical terms and put forward a working definition of 'storytelling' for the current study. This is then followed by a review on various aspects of conversational storytelling reported in previous studies including the actions implemented through storytelling, the special turn-taking organization, the serially ordered components, and the interactive nature of storytelling.

Section 2.3 then reviewed studies of recipient's participation in storytelling, an aspect that is central to the current study. The first subsection (2.3.1) introduced how 'knowing story recipient' and 'unknowing story recipient' are characterized differently in previous studies. Examples from previous studies were also used to illustrate that story recipients' different epistemic statuses not only influence how the teller would tell the story but also affect how story recipient responds to the story told so far. The second subsection (2.3.2) then reviewed studies on recipients' specific responding actions that are consequential to the the progression of a storytelling. This section gave a detailed review on various forms of recipients' responsive actions that have been studied including recipients' responses that may trigger side sequences.

In Section 2.4, studies examining the phenomena of 'side sequence' and 'returning' were reviewed. The classic study of Jefferson (1972) not only provided a clear characterization of 'side sequence' within the main sequence, but also laid a solid ground for the present study of 'side sequence' in storytelling sequences. More recent studies on these two phenomena were also reviewed.

Chapter 3 discussed the methodological issues for the study. Section 3.2 introduced CA's approach to data collection and transcribing as well as the methods for data analysis. Section 3.3 sketched an overall picture of the Chinese data for the present research and how data was transcribed and presented.

Chapter 4, the first main analysis chapter, presented an analysis of 'recipient-initiated side sequences'. First, the sequential organization of side sequences within the telling sequence is outlined. I started by identifying the minimal side sequence with regard to the locus where first opportunity of return may be taken up. As shown below, there are two formats of minimal side sequence within thc telling sequence:

A three-turn side sequence within telling sequence (a reproduction of Table 4)

Storyteller:		Ongoing storytelling
Recipient:	→	Side-sequence-initiating action

Contined

Storyteller:		Ongoing storytelling
Storyteller:		Orienting to recipient's action
Recipient:		Sequence closing third (SCT)
Storyteller:		Returning to halted telling

Returning occurs after storyteller's response (a reproduction of Table 5)

Storyteller:		Ongoing storytelling
Recipient:	→	Side-sequence-initiating action
Storyteller:		responding to recipient action +
		returning to halted telling

In the first table above, the storyteller's ongoing storytelling gets halted because of a responsive action by the recipient which sets up expectation for storyteller's uptake. After the storyteller responds to that action and the recipient produces a sequence-closing third, the storyteller can resume his/her halted telling. In the second table, the storyteller resumes his/her telling immediately after he/she responds to the recipient's side-sequence-initiating action. In other words, in the second table, the storyteller makes use of the response turn to resume telling in the next TCU following the response to the recipient-initiated action in the first turn of the side sequence.

These two tables explicitly present the different sequential points at which the storyteller can return to halted story. In the first format of the side sequence, as the storyteller does not opt for story return immediately after responding to the recipient, it is the story recipient who proposes to close the side sequence in the next turn (with SCT which does not contribute further talk on the topic in the side sequence), thus providing an opportunity for possible story return by the storyteller in the next turn. In the second format of side sequence, it is the storyteller who implements story return right after responding to the recipient question or other actions that initiated the side sequence, leading to a shorter route to story return.

Regarding the interactional actions that occasion the side sequences which halt a story-in-progress, the data shows several patterns. Very frequently, a side sequence occurs because the story recipient requests additional details about the story told so far. One of the findings from my data is that, when the storyteller responds to this request for details, the response is often substantial. The storyteller may even provide more information than was asked for. If the issue in question is beyond the epistemic domain of the storyteller's knowledge, he/she may also proffer certain relevant information in lieu of the requested information. It is rare for the storyteller not to orient to the recipient's request. This shows that the first turn by the recipient in the side sequence has a dual nature in that it is at once responsive and initiative. It is responsive in the sense that it responds to some aspects in the story-so-far. But they differ from other minimal responses such as continuers since they are usually non-minimal and thus usually engender further talk on the topic. In this regard the same responsive turn is also initiative in nature. In fact, these turns are often constructed as a first pair part themselves as in the adjacency pair, e.g. as questions, other-initiation, etc.. It is the initiative nature of such turns that explains the storyteller's obligation to respond to it by producing a matching response.

Although certain recipient responses are facilitative in nature (e.g. recipients' other repair, collaborative completion, and predicting of storyline), as the storyteller needs to take a turn space to deal with them (halting the ongoing telling), they still trigger side sequences. Display of stance or understanding by the recipient can also initiate a side sequence. The data shows that such displays do not only occur upon story completion; rather, during the telling sequence, story recipients will seize the opportunities available to them to offer their views, express their doubts, or show their understanding toward the story-so-far. In doing so, the story recipient is acting on a chance to establish and update intersubjectivity with the storyteller.

On-the-spot establishing and updating of intersubjectivity during the telling sequence highly reflects the fundamentally open and interactive nature of storytelling. Since what a story would finally amount to is neither absolute nor pre-determined (although it can be envisioned or projected to certain extent), the story recipient has to respond to the story in order to engage with the storyteller and make sure their understanding toward the story-so-far is aligning with the teller's perspective.

In addition, this chapter also addressed the issue of how minimal side sequence may be developed into an expanded one. The findings show that the expanded side sequence can result from dealing with contingencies that arise in the side sequence. Or it can be achieved through 'sequence design', i.e. the side sequence is designed to be a complex one in which the first turn is used by the story recipient to prepare for an upcoming action in further turns. Furthermore, the story teller may also re-open the already closed side sequence thus leading to a sequence expansion. The present research not only identified various actions of story recipients that may trigger side sequences, but also differentiated side sequences according to their complexity in terms of sequence organization (Schegloff, 2007).

In Chapter 5, the strategies and indicators of storytelling return were investigated. It was found in my case-by-case analysis of each storytelling sequence that there is no fundamental discrimination between returning devices used after minimal side sequence and expanded side sequence (except resuming search), and this chapter mainly focused on returnings after expanded side sequence.

The chapter began with the most explicit device for doing returning — repetition. Repetition clearly creates a bridge connecting the utterances before and after the side sequence, although the length of the utterance selected for repetition depends on its local interactional environment and its sequential position. The storyteller may also return to the halted telling without repetition, but just produce the next element in the story as if no interruption has taken place. It is found that this form of returning, i.e. direct continuation, most frequently occurs after relatively brief side sequences, although it also happens after some expanded side sequences. I found that, when returns are achieved through direct continuation, the discourse marker *ranhou* 'and then' is very often present. Studies of Chinese grammar and discourse have shown that the function of *ranhou* has gradually expanded from temporal conjunction to discourse marker for sequential organization in multi-unit turns. These functions make it possible for the word to connect story elements prior and subsequent to the side sequence, either temporally or sequentially.

Another lexical item found to be relevant to return is the adverb *fanzheng* 'anyway', which often signals a closing of the side sequence and projects an imminent return. Studies in Chinese discourse have shown that this adverb embodies a sense of concluding. Thus, *fanzheng*-prefaced utterances in side sequence are heard as sequencing-closing implicative. In this sense, it facilitates story return.

Sometimes, a return cannot be easily achieved. In these cases, when local contingencies interfere or the side sequence becomes lengthy, extra effort must be made by the storyteller to get back to the halted telling. For example, when the story was interrupted for several times, the teller may explicitly resist the possible side sequence initiator. And when a story was put on hold for a rather long time (e.g. several minutes), a resume search may be used by the teller.

The last section of this chapter (Section 5.3) examined possible interactional motivations for doing story return. Very often story return serves to ensure that the story arrives at its completion so the moral or climax of the story can be presented. Sometimes, when the story is being delivered to initiate a particular course of action, the purpose of the return is then to bring that course of action to completion. These two points show that story return is not a random or coincidental phenomenon. Rather, it has its own interactional import for the conversation in which the story is being told.

6.2 Contribution

Findings from the current study make three main contributions to the field of conversation analysis.

Firstly, this study contributes to the study of a less researched topic in CA. Comparing with topics such as repair, turn design, adjacency pairs, etc., which have been intensively studied, storytelling is an area which is relatively less explored. 'Story suspension' and 'story return' have not been studied together as a coherent phenomenon, although story recipients' non-minimal responses (C. Goodwin, 1986; M. Goodwin, 1997; Koike, 2009; Mandelbaum, 1987, 1989; Ochs & Capps, 2001) and 'side sequence' (Jefferson, 1972; Svennevig, 1999) have been researched in separate studies. With a focus on the examination of the main telling sequence, the current study not only sketched the organization of side sequences within the telling sequence, but also revealed an important issue during the telling sequence, i.e. the goal of these side sequences is to establish and update intersubjectivity between the storyteller and recipient. This on-spot establishing and updating of intersubjectivity and understanding is clear evidence for story recipients' active role in co-organizing storytelling, and the contingent and open nature of storytelling in conversation (C. Goodwin, 2015;

Mandelbaum, 1987, 1989).

Secondly, the current study contributes to the growing body of research in CA studies in Chinese. CA studies have being flourishing in many languages other than English (e.g. Finnish, Dutch, German, Japanese and Korean, etc). There is also a growing body of CA studies drawing on Chinese conversational data which examined final particles (Luke, 1990; Wu, 2004), repair (Luke & Zhang, 2010; Zhang, 1998, Zhang & Chan, 2013), and turn organization (Li, 2011). However, systematic studies on storytelling in Chinese are rare. In this regard, the current study fills a gap in Chinese CA studies, and opens up an avenue for further research in storytelling in Chinese.

Thirdly, the findings from the current study provide fresh materials for cross-linguistic/cultural studies. Conversation analysts have started to conduct large-scale studies across a large number of languages on a number of topics. Among them, question-response sequences in ten languages are examined (Enfield, Stivers & Levinson, 2010); other-initiated repair across languages is investigated to work out a typology of conversational structural (Dingemanse & Enfield, 2015); and the universals and cultural variation in turn-taking are also studied (Stivers, et al., 2009). My current study then contributes to possible cross-cultural and cross-linguistic comparison of the structures and functions of storytelling in conversation. For instance, the discourse marker *ranhou* 'and then' in Chinese can be compared to *and* in English and *de* 'and' in Japanese for their use in returning after side sequence. Possible social actions carried through storytelling and interactional import for story return can also be compared across languages for a better understanding of storytelling as a conversational activity in diverse linguistic and cultural contexts.

6.3 Limitation

This study has some limitations. First, the types of recipient-initiating action identified in the current study are not exhaustive (nor were they intended to be). Second, the interactional functions of returning warrant further explanation beyond what is presented here; the present study limits itself to offering more examples of stories where a particular interactional function appeared to be at play — no quantitative assessment is offered. Third, I did not systematically investigate the recipients' responses in those stories where returning is completely blocked, nor those in which the recipient's initial response is ignored by the storyteller. These phenomena likewise deserve their own detailed investigation.

6.4 Future directions

First, it would be interesting to compare recipient responses that completely block the story with those that briefly halt the story but permit that story to be resumed later. Is there a systematic difference between these two scenarios? Secondly, in terms of the overall organization of the storytelling sequence, there is still much to explore in Chinese conversations. For example, it would be interesting to investigate how stories are occasioned, and what interactional import stories may have. Thirdly, storytelling in conversation can also be analyzed from a multi-modal perspective, i.e. to incorporate the study of prosodic patterns, the bodily behavior of participants, etc. which will help get a more comprehensive picture of storytelling in conversation.

Thus, my current study takes only the first step in understanding the big picture of storytelling as an interactional phenomenon.

References

Atkinson, M., & Heritage, J. (1984). *Structures of Social Action: Studies in Conversation Analysis*. Cambridge: Cambridge University Press.

Beach, W. (2000). Inviting collaborations in stories about a woman. *Language in Society*, 29, 379-407.

Bruner, J. (1986). *Actual Minds, Possible Worlds*. Cambridge, MA: Harvard University Press.

Bruner, J. (1990). *Acts of Meaning*. Cambridge, MA: Harvard University Press.

Bruner, J. (2002). *Making Stories: Law, Literature, Life*. New York: Farrar, Straus and Giroux.

Clayman, S. (2013). Turn-constructional units and the transition relevance place. In J. Sidnell and T. Stivers (Eds.), *The Handbook of Conversation Analysis* (pp. 150-166). Oxford: Wiley-Blackwell.

Clayman, S., & Heritage, J. (2002). *The news interview: Journalists and public figures on the air*. Cambridge University Press.

Dingemanse, M., & Enfield, N. (2015). Other-initiated repair across languages: Towards a typology of conversational structures. *Open Linguistics*, 1, 96-118.

Enfield, N., Stivers, T., & Levinson, S. (2010). Question-response sequences in conversation across ten languages: An introduction. *Journal of Pragmatics*, 42(10), 2615-2619.

Fang, M. (2000). Reduced conjunctions as discourse markers. *Studies of the Chinese Language*, 5, 459-480.

Goffman, E. (1974). *Frame Analysis: An Essay on the Organization of Experience*. Cambridge: Harvard University Press.

Goffman, E. (1983). The interaction order: American Sociological Association, 1982 presidential address. *American sociological review*, 1-17.

Goodwin, C. (1979). The interactive construction of a sentence in natural conversation. In G. Psathas (Ed.), *Everyday language: Studies in ethnomethodology* (pp. 97-121). New York: Irvington.

Goodwin, C. (1984). Notes on Story Structure and the Organization of Participation. In M. Atkinson and J. Heritage (Eds.), *Structures of Social Action* (pp. 225-246). Cambridge: Cambridge University Press.

Goodwin, C. (1986). Audience Diversity, Participation and Interpretation. *Text*, 6(3), 283-316.

Goodwin, C. (1986). Between and within: Alternative sequential treatments of continuers and assessments. *Human Studies, 9,* 205-217.

Goodwin, C. (2015). Storytelling as an Interactive Process. In: A. De Fina and A. Georgakopoulon (Eds.). *The Handbook of Narrative Analysis* (pp. 197-218) Oxford: Wiley Blackwell.

Goodwin, M. (1993). Tactical Uses of Stories: Participation frameworks within girls' and boys' disputes. In D. Tannen (Ed.), *Gender and Conversational Interaction* (pp. 110-142). New York: Oxford University Press.

Goodwin, M. (1997). By-Play: Negotiating Evaluation in Story-Telling. In G. R. Guy, C. Feagin, D. Schiffrin, and J. Baugh (Eds), *Towards a Social Science of Language: Papers in Honour of William Labov. 2: Social Interaction and Discourse Structures* (pp. 77-102). Amsterdam/Philadelphia: Benjamins.

Heritage, J. & Atkinsan, J. M. (1984). Introduction. In J.M. Atkinson, and J. Heritage (Eds). *Structures of Social Action: Studies in Conversation Analysis* (pp. 1-15). Cambridge: Cambridge University Press.

Heritage, J., & Raymond, G. (2005). The Terms of Agreement: Indexing Epistemic Authority and Subordination in Assessment Sequences. *Social Psychology Quarterly*, 68, 15-38.

Houtkoop, H., & Mazeland, H. (1985). Turns and discourse units in everyday conversation. *Journal of Pragmatics*, 9(5), 595-620.

Hutchby, I., & Wooffitt, R. (2008). *Conversation Analysis*. (2nd ed.). Cambridge: Polity.

Jefferson, G. (1972). Side sequences. In D. N. Sudnow (Ed.), *Studies in social interaction* (pp. 294-333). New York: Free Press.

Jefferson, G. (1978). Sequential Aspects of Storytelling in Conversation. In J. Schenkein (Ed.), *Studies in the Organization of Conversational Interaction* (pp. 219-248). New York: Academic Press.

Jefferson, G. (1980). On "trouble-premonitory" response to inquiry. *Sociological Inquiry,* 50, 153-185.

Jefferson, G. (1981) "Caveat Speaker": A preliminary exploration of shift-implicative recipiency in the articulation of topic. End of grant report to the (British) Social Science Research Council on the articulation of topic in conversation.

Jefferson, G. (1987). On exposed and embedded correction in conversation. In G. Button and J. Lee (Eds.), *Talk and social organization* (pp. 86-100). Clevedon, UK: Multilingual Matters.

Jefferson, G. (1988). On the sequential organization of troubles talk in ordinary conversation. *Social Problems,* 35, 418-442.

Jefferson, G. (1993). Caveat speaker: Preliminary notes on recipient topic-shift implicature. *Research on language and social interaction,* 26, 1-30.

Jefferson, G., & Lee, J. (1981). The rejection of advice: Managing the problematic convergence of a "troubles-telling" and a "service encounter". *Journal of Pragmatics*, 5(5), 399-422.

Kelly, J. & Local, J. (1989). On the Use of General Phonetic Techniques in Handling Conversational Material. In D. Roger, and P. Bull (Eds), *Conversation* (pp. 197-212). Clevedon: Multilingual Matters.

Koenig, C. (2005). Question initiated oblique sequences: A recipient's practice in multi-unit turn environments. Unpublished manuscript.

Koike, C. (2009). *Interaction in storytelling in Japanese conversations: An analysis of story recipients' questions*, PhD dissertation, University of California, Los Angeles.

Kuo, Sai-hua. (2002). Cooperation and Competition in Collaborative Narration: Analyzing Storytelling in Taiwanese Young Adults' Conversations. In Lily I-wen Su, Chinfa Lien, and Kawai Chui (Eds.), *Form and Function: Linguistics Studies in Honor of Shuanfan Huang* (pp. 131-151). Taipei: Crane Publishing.

Labov, W. (1972). *Language in the Inner city: Studies in the Black English Vernacular.* Philadelphia: University of Pennsylvania Press.

Labov, W., & Waletzky, J. (1967). Narrative analysis. In J. Helm (Ed.), *Essays on the verbal and visual arts* (pp. 12-44). Seattle: U. of Washington Press. Reprinted in *Journal of Narrative and Life History*, 7, 1-38.

Lerner, G. (1991). On the Syntax of Sentences in Progress. *Language in Society*, 20, 441-458.

Lerner, G. (1992). Assisted Storytelling: Deploying Shared Knowledge as a Practical Matter. *Qualitative Sociology*, 15, 247-271.

Lerner, G. (1996). On the "semi-permeable" character of grammatical units in conversation: Conditional entry into the turn space of another speaker. In E. Ochs, E. Schegloff, and S. Thompson (Eds.), *Interaction and Grammar*, (pp. 238-276). Cambridge: Cambridge University Press.

Lerner, G. (2004). Collaborative Turn Sequences. In G. Lerner (Ed.), *Conversation Analysis: Studies from the First Generation.* Amsterdam: John Benjamins.

Li, C. & Thompson, S. (1981). *Mandarin Chinese: A functional reference grammar.* Berkley, Los Angeles, London: University of California Press.

Li, Xiaoting. (2011). *Syntax, Prosody and Body Movements in Turn Organization in Everyday Face-to-Face conversation.* PhD dissertation, Peking University.

Local, J. (2004). Getting back to prior talk: and-uh(m) as a back-connecting device. In E. Couper-Kuhlen, and C. Ford (Eds.), *Sound patterns in interaction: Cross-linguistic studies of phonetics and prosody for conversation* (pp. 377-400). Amsterdam/Philadelphia: John Benjamins Publishing.

Luke, K. K. (1990). *Utterance Particles in Cantonese Conversation.* Amsterdam/Philadelphia: John Benjamins.

Luke, K. K. & Zhang, W. (2010). Insertion as a self-repair device and its interactional motivations in Chinese conversation. *Chinese Language and Discourse*, 1(2), 153-182.

Mandelbaum, J. (1987). *Recipient-driven storytelling in conversation.* PhD dissertation, The University of Texas at Austin.

Mandelbaum, J. (1989). Interpersonal Activities in Conversational Storytelling. *Western Journal of Speech Communication*, 53(2), 114-126.

Mandelbaum, J. (1993). Assigning responsibility in conversational storytelling: The interactional construction of reality. *Text,* 13, 247-266.

Mandelbaum, J. (2013). Storytelling in Conversation. In J. Sidnell and T. Stivers (Eds.), *The Handbook of Conversation Analysis* (pp. 492-507). Oxford: Wiley-Blackwell.

Mazeland, H., & Huiskes, M. (2001). Dutch 'but' as a sequential conjunction. In M. Selting and E. Couper-Kuhlen (Eds.), *Studies in interactional linguistics* (pp. 141-169). Amsterdam/ Philadelphia: John Benjamins Publishing.

Miracle, W. C. (1989). Hao: A Chinese Discourse Marker. In B. Music et al. (Eds), *Papers from the 25th Regional Meeting of the Chicago Linguistic Society, Part 2: Parasession on Language in Context* (pp. 213–27). Chicago, IL: University of Chicago Linguistics Department.

Miracle, W. C. (1991). *Discourse Markers in Mandarin Chinese*, PhD dissertation, The Ohio State University.

Monzoni, C. & Drew, P. (2009). Inter-interactional contexts of story-interventions by non-knowledgeable story recipients in (Italian) multi-person interaction. *Journal of Pragmatics*, 41, 197–218.

Norrick, N. (1997). Twice-told tales: Collaborative narration of familiar stories. *Language and Society,* 26, 199-220.

Norrick, N. (1998). Retelling stories in spontaneous conversation. *Discourse Processes*, 25, 75-97.

Norrick, N. (2000). *Conversational narrative: Storytelling in everyday talk*. Amsterdam: Benjamins.

Norrick, N. (2004). Humor, tellability, and conarration in conversational storytelling. *Text*, 24, 79–111.

Norrick, N. (2013). Narratives of vicarious experience in conversation. *Language in Society*, 42, 1-22.

Ochs, E., & Capps, L. (2001). *Living Narrative: Creating Lives in Everyday Storytelling*. Cambridge: Harvard University Press.

Ochs, E., Schegloff, E., & Thompson, S. (Eds.). (1996). *Interaction and grammar*. Cambridge, England: Cambridge University Press.

Ottesjö, C. (2005). *To continue and to resume: A study of coherence-creating practices in everyday multiparty conversations,* PhD dissertation, Göteborg University.

Owen, M. (1985). The conversational functions of anyway. *The Nottingham Linguistic Circular*, 14, 72-90.

Park, I. (2010). Marking an impasse: the use of anyway as a sequence-closing device. *Journal of Pragmatics*, 42(12), 3283-3299.

Polanyi, L. (1985). *Telling the American story: A structural and cultural analysis of conversational storytelling*. Norwood, NJ: Albex publishers.

Pomerantz, A. (1984). Agreeing and disagreeing with assessments: Some features of preferred/dispreferred turn shapes. In M. Atkinson & J. Heritage (Eds.), *Structures of social action: Studies in conversation analysis* (pp. 57-101). Cambridge, England: Cambridge University Press.

Rauniomaa, M. (2008). *Recovery through repetition: Returning to prior talk and taking a stance in American-English and Finnish conversations,* PhD dissertation, University of

Oulu.

Sacks, H. (1974a). An analysis of the course of a joke's telling in conversation. In R. Bauman and J. F. Sherzer (Eds.), *Explorations in the Ethnography of Speaking* (pp. 337-353). Cambridge: Cambridge University Press.

Sacks, H. (1974b). Some consideration of a story told in ordinary conversations. *Poetics*, 15, 127-138.

Sacks, H. (1978). Some technical considerations of a dirty joke. In J. Schenkein (Ed.), *Studies in the Organization of Conversational Interaction* (pp. 249-269). New York: Academic Press.

Sacks, H. (1986). Some Considerations of a Story Told in Ordinary Conversations. *Poetics: International Review for the Theory of Literature,* 15(1-2), 127-138.

Sacks, H. (1995a). *Lectures on Conversation, Vol. 1.* Oxford: Blackwell.

Sacks, H. (1995b). *Lectures on Conversation, Vol. 2.* Oxford: Blackwell.

Sacks, H., Schegloff, E., & Jefferson, G. (1974). A Simplest Systematics for the Organization of Turn-taking for Conversation. *Language*, 50(4), 696-735.

Sarbin, T. (1986). *Narrative psychology: the storied nature of human conduct.* New York: Praeger.

Schegloff, E. (1968). Sequencing in conversational openings. *American anthropologist*, 70(6), 1075-1095.

Schegloff, E. (1982). Discourse as an Interactional Achievement: Some Uses of 'uh huh' and Other Things That Come Between Sentences. In D. Tannen (Ed.), *Analyzing Discourse: Text and Talk* (pp. 71-93). Washington D.C.: Georgetown University Press.

Schegloff, E. (1996). Confirming Allusions: Toward an Empirical Account of Action. *American Journal of Sociology*, 102(1), 161–216.

Schegloff, E. (1997). 'Narrative Analysis' Thirty Years Later. *Journal of Narrative and Life History*, 7(1-4), 97-106.

Schegloff, E. (2007). *Sequence organization in interaction: A primer in conversation analysis.* Cambridge: Cambridge University press.

Schegloff, E., Jefferson, G., & Sacks, H. (1977). The preference for self-correction in the organization of repair in conversation. *Language*, 53, 361-382.

Schegloff, M. (1982). Discourse as an interactional achievement: Some uses of 'uh huh' and other things that come between sentences. In D. Tannen (Ed.), *Georgetown University Roundtable on Languages and Linguistics l98l; Analyzing Discourse: Text and Talk* (pp.

71-93). Georgetown: Georgetown University Press.

Schegloff, M. (1997). 'Narrative Analysis' Thirty Years Later. *Journal of Narrative and Life History*, 7(1-4), 97-106.

Sidnell, J., & Stivers, T. (2013). *Handbook of Conversation Analysis*. Oxford: Wiley-Blackwell.

Siromaa, M. (2012). Resonance in conversational second stories: A dialogic resource for stance taking. *Text & Talk, 32*, 525-545.

Stivers, T. (2008). Stance, alignment, and affiliation during storytelling: When nodding is a token of affiliation. *Research on Language and Social Interaction, 41*, 31-57.

Stivers, T., Enfield, N., Brown, P., Englert, C., Hayashi, M., Heinemann, T., Hoyman, G., Rossano, F., de Ruiter, J.P. Yoon, K., & Levinson, S. (2009). Universals and cultural variation in turn-taking in conversation. *Proceedings of the National Academy of Sciences*, 106(26), 10587-92.

Sutinen, M. (2008). *But and anyway resumptions as a strategy for managing digressions in conversational storytelling and other extended turns,* Master thesis, University of Oulu.

Sutinen, M. (2014). Negotiating favourable conditions for resuming suspended activities. In P. Haddington, T. Keisanen, L. Mondada, and M. Nevile (Eds.), *Multiactivity in Social Interaction: Beyond multitasking* (pp. 137-166). Amsterdam/Philadelphia: John Benjamins Publishing.

Svennevig, J. (1999). *Getting acquainted in conversation: a study of initial interactions*. Amsterdam/Philadelphia: John Benjamins Publishing.

Terasaki, A. (2004). Pre-announcement sequences in conversation. In G. Lerner (Ed.), *Conversation analysis: studies from the first generation* (pp. 171-239). Amsterdam: John Benjamins.

Thornborrow, J., & Coates, J. (Eds.). (2005). *The Sociolinguistics of Narratires (Vol. 6)*. Amsterdam; Philadelphia: John Berjamins Pub.

Wang, Y., Tsai, P., Goodman, D., & Lin, M. (2010). Agreement, acknowledgment, and alignment: The discourse-pragmatic functions of hao and dui in taiwan mandarin conversation. *Discourse Studies*, 12(2), 241-267.

Wong, J. (2000). Repetition in conversation: A look at "first and second sayings". *Research on Language and Social Interaction*, 33(4), 407-424.

Wu, Ruey-Jiuan. (2004). *Stance in Talk: A conversation analysis of Mandarin final particles*. Amsterdam/Philadelphia: John Benjamins.

Yasui, E. (2011). *Negotiating story entry: A micro-analytic study of storytelling projection in*

English and Japanese, PhD dissertation, The University of Texas at Austin.

Zhang, W. (1998). *Repair in Chinese Conversation*. PhD dissertation, The University of Hong Kong.

Zhang, W. & Chan, A. (2013). Self-repair in Mandarin and Cantonese: delaying the next item due in casual conversation and news interview. In Y. Pan and D. Z. Kádár (Eds.), *Chinese Discourse and Interaction: Theory and Practice* (pp. 35-57). CT: Equinox.

Zhao, Y. R., & Zhao, Y. (2014). A corpus-based discourse analysis of conversational storytelling in Chinese adults. *Chinese Language and Discourse*, 5(1), 53-78.

毕永峨 .2010. 语言使用语法化 [M]// 语言与认知 . 台北：台大出版中心 .

董正存 .2008. 情态副词“反正”的用法及相关问题研究 [J]. 语文研究 (2): 12-22.

吕叔湘 .1980. 现代汉语八百词 [M]. 北京：商务印书馆 .

许家金 .2009. 汉语自然会话中“然后”的话语功能研究 [J]. 外语研究 (114): 9-15.

Appendixes

Appendix i : Consent form

录音同意书

本人 __________ 同意□　不同意□　在日常生活中接受录像及录音，并明白录像及录音的内容只用作研究用途，所有姓名等可指认相关信息将被隐去或使用化名代替。

参与人员姓名：__________

参与人员签署：__________

日期：__________________

研究人员姓名：__________

研究人员签署：__________

日期：__________________

Appendix ii : Transcription conventions

Developed by Gail Jefferson (Atkinson and Heritage, 1984)

Notation	Meaning
A: xx [xxx] B: [yyy]yy	Square brackets are used to indicate simultaneous or overlapping speech. The left and right hand bracket indicates the onset and the end of the overlapping utterance.
A: xxxx = B: = yyyy	The equal sign indicates latching between two speakers when there is no interval between the change of speakership
A: xx [xxxx = B: [yy A: = xxxx	In this case, the equal sign is used for transcription convenience when one speaker turn is broken into two or more lines especially in the presence of overlapped utterances.
xxxx	Underlined parts means those parts are emphasized or stressed.
(.)	A dot within parentheses indicates a very short pause (less than 0.1 second)
(n)	n in the parentheses shows the length of the pause in seconds
.	A dot indicates a falling intonation, but not necessarily the end of a sentence
,	A comma indicates a level intonation, and not necessarily in the middle of a sentence
?	A question mark indicates a rising intonation, not necessarily after a question
° xxxx °	A pair of degree signs indicates a stretch of quieter talk in contrast to its surrounding utterances
↑ ↓	An upward arrow indicates a noticeable rising shift in intonation
:	A colon indicates the lengthening of prior sound. The more the colons, the longer the lengthening is.
-	A dash indicates an abrupt cut-off of the prior turn or sound.
.hh	One or more "h" s preceded by a dot indicate inhalation
(( ))	Double parentheses are used to enclose a description of the non-verbal aspects of the talk
> xxxx <	An utterance delivered at a quicker pace relative to the surrounding talk is enclosed in the "greater than" and "less than" signs
(guess)	The words within a single bracket indicate the transcriber' s best guess at an unclear utterance.
CAPITALS	Words in capitals mark a section of speech noticeably louder than that surrounding it.
→	Arrows in the left margin point to specific parts of an extract discussed in the text.

Appendix iii: Abbreviation in gloss

ASP	Aspect marker
BA	Pretransitive marker
CL	Classifier
COMP	Complement
INJT	Interjection
NEG	Negatives
ONo	Onomatopoeic word
PRT	The Particle De and sentence final particles
Q	Question particle

Acknowledgements

This book is based on my unpublished PhD thesis. First, I am grateful to my supervisor Dr. Zhang Wei for her guidance and encouragement during the past ten years. Dr. Zhang brought me to the world of CA and taught me how to use such a powerful toolkit to analyze and understand human social interaction and language in use. I truly admire her passion toward academics and strong belief in CA.

I would like to extend my sincere thanks to the Panel of Examiners for my PhD thesis. The questions and comments from Professor Tao Hongyin, Dr. Wu Dongying Doreen and Dr. Fang Chengyu Alex have let me think more thoroughly and better position my study among the existing literature. I am also very grateful to Dr. Yan Xiu Jackie and Dr. Li Bin, members of the Qualifying Panel of my PhD candidature, for their invaluable advice and comments on my qualifying and annual reports.

I wish to express my deep gratitude to professors at UCLA. I am thankful to my advisor Professor Charles Goodwin during my visit. I have greatly benefited from his instruction in discourse analysis, especially from his expertise in multi-modal analysis. I also wish to thank Professor John Heritage, Professor Steven Clayman, Professor Tao Hongyin, Professor Tanya Stivers, and Professor Marjorie Goodwin for their intensive teaching and training in classes and data sessions, and their inspiring comments on my works.

I thank the Department of Linguistics and Translation at City University of Hong Kong for providing me with a generous scholarship to support my PhD study and offering me funding to visit UCLA and attend international conferences. My special thanks go to Professor Luke Kang Kwong, Dr. Wu Ruey-jiuan Regina, and Dr. Li Xiaoting, for their critical comments on my conference presentation of 'storytelling resumption' which developed into one of the main analysis chapters of the current book.

I wish to express my sincere thanks to the College of Foreign Languages and Cultures at Xiamen University. Our department and college have provided us with unexceptionable working atmosphere. The publication of this book is strongly supported by Professor Jiang Guiying and Professor Li Meihua. My thanks also go to Dr. Zhang Kunkun for reading through the draft of this book and giving me invaluable advice and to Ms. Wang Yangfan for the editing work. Without them, it is impossible for me to publish this book.

Last but not least, I wish to thank my families and friends for their long-lasting love and warm care. I am indebted to all the participants in the recorded conversations, with which I continuously explore the unknown world with curiosity.